Dairyland

A NOVEL BY
JAMIE GODFREY

Jamie Godfrey
202 Brunswick Street
Jersey City, NJ 07302

First edition: March 2014

Library of Congress Control Number: 2014900761

Godfrey, Jamie
    Dairyland / Jamie Godfrey
    ISBN 978-0-578-13638-7

PRINTED IN THE UNITED STATES OF AMERICA

Contents

*For anyone who has fallen down,
got back up, dusted themselves off,
and just kept going.*

cheesy |ˈCHēzē|
adjective (cheesier, cheesiest)
1 like cheese in taste, smell, or consistency: *a pungent, cheesy sauce.*
2 informal cheap, unpleasant, or blatantly inauthentic: *a big cheesy grin* | *cheesy motel rooms.*

Welcome Back

A patchwork of tan colored cornfields lay scattered across the horizon. Crystals were forming on the airplane window as I tried to guess what part of the state we were over at that moment. It had been two years since I made the trip home to see everyone.

"Another?" asked the flight attendant. I nodded and took the mini vodka bottle from her hand. She in turn took the debit card from mine. Somehow, at 10 A.M., I found it acceptable to drink alcohol. Maybe it was being thousands of feet off the ground that made it ok to consume that magnificent, clear, burning liquid. The normal conventions didn't apply up there.

Minutes later, the plane landed and slowly made its way to the Dane County Regional Airport. I handed the empty bottles and plastic cup to the flight attendant with a smile. I collected my things and exited. Inside the airport, I ran to the bathroom, something about going on the plane skeeved me out. And I always feared if the plane crashed, that's where they'd find me, in that little, tiny airplane port-a-potty, covered in pee, holding my junk.

There she was. My mother. Standing at the base of the escalators, wiping back a tear. Nervously, I smiled as I inched closer to her. Before I could clear out of the way, she ran up and hugged me and planted a kiss on my cheek. I could smell her lipstick and wiped the contact site.

"You've been drinking!"

"Good to see you, too."

"C'mon!" she said, grabbing my arm and leading me in the direction of the baggage claim. "Good flight?"

"Yup," I said.

"Why do you wait so long to come home?"

"Really?" I said as she shook her head at me. The carousel started to move. Black, grey and navy bags began to drift by. Soon, there was my bright orange suitcase.

"You still have the case I bought you!" she said with pride. She knew my fondness for the color orange and was particularly proud to have found a bright orange suitcase for me.

Outside, the air was unexpectedly crisp. I wished I hadn't packed my coat in my suitcase and I was too lazy to retrieve it. "Aren't you cold?" she asked, motherly tone in place. I nodded. I got in her car and turned on the heated seat option.

The sky was grey and overcast. The trees had lost all of their leaves, creating quilts of yellow, red and orange to cover the grass. It was midway between fall and winter. I let out a sigh.

"Are you hungry?" Mom asked, already knowing the answer to that question.

"You know me. I can always eat." She turned the radio on to the oldies station.

"Great! Let's go to Chili's." Not exactly my first choice for lunch, but I wasn't in a position to turn down free food.

My mom looked older since I saw her last, I thought. I could see the start of liver spots on her hands and one or two stray strands of grey hair. That made me sad. She had settled into middle age with grace, however, with a second coming as a successful real estate agent after a career consisting of a string of odd jobs. I admired people who woke up late in life and found their calling. It seemed more deserved than those who discovered it earlier.

"Welcome to Chili's," said this overweight guy with a visible booger in his nose and fingerprints all over the lenses of his glasses. Oh, God, I thought. We were seated at a table near the windows. I could see the traffic flowing in and out of the Barnes & Noble parking lot. My menu stuck to the table.

"What are you going to get?" Mom asked with enthusiasm.

"I don't know."

"I don't even have to look. I know what I'm having." I knew what it was. Steak, cooked until it was uniformly brown and flavorless, baked potato with cheese and sour cream and an iceberg lettuce salad with ranch dressing. I really wanted a cocktail more than anything. But, I settled on the bacon cheeseburger sliders, which gave me instant asspiss.

"You feeling ok?" she asked as I returned from the bathroom.

"My stomach is bothering me a little."

"So! Talk to me! Tell me what's been going on out in New York."

"Nothing really."

"You have nothing to tell me?" It was coming. I needed to tell her. Rip it off like a Band-Aid.

"Well," my voice cracked a little. "I lost my job." The smile fell from her face.

"Oh, Kyle. Why?"

"I don't know. Just wasn't working out. Please don't say anything to anyone."

"I won't. But, what are you going to do?"

"I will figure it out. I always do." The check came and Mom took out a hundred-dollar bill and set it on top of it. She always seemed to pay for everything with hundred-dollar bills, which was an upgrade as she used to pay for everything with a check. It was embarrassing. She slid another one across the table to me. "What's this for?" I asked.

"A little to help you out." I quickly put the money in my wallet. I didn't want anyone to see me and judge me. Look at that guy taking money from his mom. I wonder if he lives in her basement. Or is about to? I could imagine people's thoughts.

"Thank you," I said, looking at the tile-covered table.

We got back into her car and headed towards Mineral Point, my hometown. It is a sleepy little burg, about forty-five minutes from Madison. I knew the drive well. I had made it a thousand times when I lived there.

Miners from Cornwall, England founded the town. The hills around it were rich with lead. Also in the ground, was a surplus of limestone, which the settlers used to build the majority of the town's buildings. Pendarvis, the tourist destination with its historical buildings and manicured lawns, was on Shake Rag Street. Legend has it that the wives of the miners would wave and shake their dishrags to let the men know that food was ready.

Because of its proximity to Madison, and it was three and a half hours to Chicago, it attracted a large artist population. I loved the duality of the agrarian and artisan coexisting, potters, weavers, painters and farmers living side-by-side.

Mom turned off Highway 151 at an exit that was new since last time I was back. As we made our way through town, towards my grandmother's house (I stayed with her whenever I was back ever since my grandfather died), a flood of memories washed over my mind. It was all so familiar and yet none of it felt like home.

A First for Everything
(Memory #1)

The summer before I began my time at Architecture School, I worked at the local grocery store. I started there two years earlier to finance my piano lessons. Boring as it was, ringing up groceries was pretty much the only source of income for high school students in the area.

At the edge of the counter I was standing behind was a stack of the local newspaper, *The Democrat Tribune*. On the cover was a photo of older man and woman and a young guy. He caught my eye. They had opened a new restaurant in the old Walker House building. Hmmm, I thought. Looks like I need to go there for dinner.

I looked up from the newspaper to find the guy from the photo standing directly in front of me. "Hello," he said, setting a carton of half and half and three lemons on the counter. He was beautiful. Perfectly chiseled face, flawlessly tanned skin, crystal blue eyes, immaculately coifed sandy blond hair and chic tortoise shell glasses that rounded out the look. He couldn't be much older than me, I thought.

"Hello," I said nervously. I rang up the items and he handed me a twenty-dollar bill. He was holding a motorcycle helmet in his hands. I gave him his change and he put the items into his backpack.

"See you," he said, in a slightly flirty voice. I watched him get onto the back of a crotch rocket and zip out of the parking lot. I was lost. I had to see him again. I held the newspaper up to my friend Melissa across at the other checkout lane. She was in her late thirties, hopelessly single and my best friend at the time. Often after work, we'd take a frozen pizza and videos to her house. She was the first person I told I am gay.

"You want to go to dinner?" I asked. She took the newspaper from my hands and smiled.

"Evan, huh?" she said. "Sure. Let's go Friday night." We got paid on Friday, so that made sense. But it was Tuesday. What was I going to do until Friday? I put the newspaper in my bag and fifty cents into the register.

The Walker House was this sprawling three story limestone building tucked into the hillside behind it. It had been an inn, bar, restaurant and hotel on and off for decades since being erected in the 1800s. There were several cars in the parking lot. That's a good sign, I thought. Melissa was so excited to try out the restaurant. I was so excited to see Evan again. We entered the building and made our way to the second floor, which contained the lounge/bar and the restaurant.

The dining room was dressed in the typical burgundy and hunter green so commonly found in Midwest décor. There was a large stone fireplace in the middle of the room. I wished it were winter so we could sit in front of a roaring fire, eating our dinner and me flirting with Evan.

"Two?" the hostess asked us while grabbing menus from the podium. Melissa nodded with excitement. In a town of 2,000 people, a new restaurant was a big deal. We were led past the fireplace, to a cozy table by a window. Fresh cut daises sat in plain glass vases on each table.

"This is so nice," Melissa said, taking her seat at the table.

"Your server will with you shortly," said the hostess as she handed us each a menu. I left Melissa to study it with devout concentration. I scanned the room for Evan. Where was he? Oh, no! I thought. What if he's not working? It was Friday night. He had to be working.

"Kyle!" exclaimed Jodi, a former classmate of mine.

"I had no idea you worked here," I said. I knew now I had a way to get to Evan.

"Yeah, just until September before I head to the UW." Most of my classmates were headed to Madison for college. I was the lone person going clear across the state to Milwaukee. "Do you know what you want?" Evan, I thought.

"I'll have chicken saltimbocca," said Melissa eagerly.

"I'll have the angel hair pasta with cream sauce," I said. I watched Jodi walk away. Through the swinging door, as she returned to the kitchen, I could see Evan standing at the stove. "He's here!" I whispered to Melissa. She immediately turned and looked at the kitchen door. "Don't look!"

"I think you should ask Jodi to talk to him for you."

"I will. But what should I say?" Jodi returned with our Diet Cokes. I decided to spill it. "Your boss is hot," I blurted out, realizing that I hadn't yet come out to her. She quickly grinned, piecing it together.

"I'll see what I can do," she said. A wave of nervousness washed over me. I felt pale and flushed at the same time. What would I say? I was so not good at this.

"He said he'll come out and say hi in a few minutes," Jodi said, setting our food down. Melissa kicked me under the table with a squeal. She loved living vicariously through anyone else's experiences. While delicious, I could barely eat my pasta because of my nerves. Every other bite, I would hit a green peppercorn. The heat mixed with the cream and garlic was perfectly balanced. I imagined Evan cooking for me every night. I could get used to this, I thought.

The kitchen door swung open and there he was, headed in our direction. He wore a pink polo shirt and a waist apron that went down to his ankles. I could see a bulge behind the apron. He extended his hand. "Hi! I'm Evan."

"Kyle," I said, voice cracking. "And this is my friend, Melissa." He shook her hand as well.

"How is your meal?" he asked in the most beautiful voice. Of course, even his voice was beautiful.

"It's amazing. Where did you learn to cook?"

"I just graduated from MATC." I had several friends going to the same technical college in Madison. I calculated that he was probably around 22. I being 18, made him seem so much older than me.

"You are very talented," Melissa added.

"Well, I should get back to the kitchen. Very nice meeting you both," he said, placing his hand on my shoulder before exiting.

"He's so hot!" whispered Melissa with excitement. Yes, yes he was.

The following morning, I worked the early shift at the grocery store. I saw Evan's motorcycle pull into the parking lot. He stopped out of view. I waited nervously for him to enter the store. When he did, he came directly to the checkout counter. I could see a bouquet of white tulips in his hands.

"For you," he said, offering them to me.

"Thank you," I said.

"Would you like to go on a date with me?" Was this really happening? Me? On a date? With him? I nodded. "Great! Are you free tonight? You can come to the restaurant after we close." It was set. I agreed to meet him there. He told me not to eat beforehand.

That night, I sat in my car until the last patron left the restaurant. I climbed the stairs and asked for Evan. He entered the dining room and said he'd be done in five minutes. I watched the waitresses stack chairs onto the tables and vacuum underneath them. I wandered back out into the reception area and looked at the old photographs on the walls from when Mineral Point was in its prime.

"C'mere you," a voice beckoned from behind me. I turned and Evan took both of my hands and led me into the room opposite the dining room. It was a smaller dining room that wasn't used. On the floor was a tablecloth with two plates, a bottle of wine and candles all around it. "I made you a picnic," he said, my heart melting.

I sat on the tablecloth and he handed me a glass of wine. I never drank in high school and wasn't used to the alcohol. My face was instantly flush. He handed me a plate full of fried chicken, mashed potatoes and a slice of cornbread. We sat in silence, enjoying our comfort food. I took a sip of wine and he leaned in and kissed me. I'll never forget that kiss.

Going South Up North (Memory #2)

All throughout high school, I was jealous of my straight peers. I would sit by myself in the cafeteria and overhear gossip about going steady and making out and the occasional sex story. That didn't interest me so much as just having a boyfriend and the validation that would come from having one. Look at me. I'm ok. I'm attractive. Someone else thinks so.

Things with Evan couldn't have gone better. We saw each other almost daily, after each of our shifts ended. Some nights I would stay over in his small room above the restaurant. I would fall asleep naked next to him, having just made love, the cool summer night air floating over our bodies. He smelled like Armani cologne and Listerine. I was so in love with him. I couldn't believe he was mine.

September was looming. I didn't want the summer to end. I had waited years for this and wasn't about to give it up. Milwaukee was two and a half hours away. Not exactly a commute to make every day to run a restaurant. Evan said he wasn't opposed to moving to Milwaukee with me, that there were plenty of opportunities at restaurants there. I daydreamed about what domestic life with Evan would be like, me at the drafting table, him coming in after dinner service, kissing the top of my head and hugging me from behind.

"Let's get away from here," he said, caressing my chest in bed.

"You mean like a vacation?"

"My parents and I would go to Mackinac Island in Michigan every summer. We would stay at the Grand Hotel."

"Never heard of it."

"It's great. No cars are allowed on the island. You have to take a ferry over and then everything is horse-drawn."

"Sounds cool." It was settled. The following week, Evan temporarily traded in his motorcycle for his mother's Acura and we began the long journey north. For the better part of the trip, we held hands, wind blowing through our hair, R.E.M. on the CD player. It dawned on me that Evan and I had never said we loved one another.

We pulled into a sketchy looking Holiday Inn for the night, deciding to take the last leg of the trip in the morning and catch the ferry first thing. The hallway smelled vaguely of chlorine and wet towels. In our room we found that it had a vibrating bed. Having a fondness for anything kitschy, I ran to the front desk to exchange bills for quarters. I was hoping that it would inspire some adult playtime, but it sent us both right to sleep.

The next morning, we stopped at a gas station for coffees and croissants and set out to complete the final part of the trip. We pulled into the parking lot for the ferry, just in time. Upon arriving on the island side, we took a horse-drawn carriage to the hotel.

With its sprawling veranda, yellow awnings and red geraniums everywhere, the Grand Hotel came into view. "Wow," I said. "It's beautiful." Inside the hotel, Evan went to the front desk to check in. I stood and stared at my reflection in the glossy black and white checkered floor. I felt completely underdressed and out of place. Evan came from money. His father was some big shot in Madison at a medical supply company. I came from a line of farmers and factory workers.

"Let's go," he said, room key in hand. We only had our backpacks and garment bags so we didn't need the porter. In a rare public display of affection, he took my hand in his and we headed for the elevators.

Our room was covered in bright pink floral chintz. There were two beds with gauzy canopies above each. Gold gilded mirrors hung above both beds. A giant bouquet of pink carnations was placed on the marble table between them. I went over to the window and drew the shades. We had a perfect view of Lake Huron.

"This will be the sex bed," Evan said flopping down on it. "The other is the sleep bed." I ran over and jumped on top of him, kissing him as he took off my polo shirt.

After we were finished making love, I went into the bathroom to shower. "Even the soap is made from geraniums!" I shouted out to Evan. He joined me a few moments later.

"What do you want to do tonight?" he asked, soaping up my back.

"I don't care. I just want to be with you."

"Let's get dressed up, have dinner here in the hotel and then go out on the island for a drink." I agreed.

We each brought with us one suit. It was policy in the formal dining room. My suit was a light grey one my mom had bought me for my high school graduation. Evan's was a pale olive Armani one. My wares embarrassed me but Evan assured me I was beautiful.

Dinner was outstanding. Unlike anything I had ever experienced. From the formal service to the quality of the food, I was blown away. And I was with Evan. He convinced the waiter to serve us wine even though I refused to show my driver's license. I told the waiter I left it in the room. Evan showed his and assured him we were the same age.

Tipsy from the wine, we went back to the room to change out of our suits. Evan was in worse shape than I was despite having the same amount of alcohol. We both changed into khaki shorts and polo shirts and headed out to continue our evening.

We came upon what looked more like a house party than a bar. "Let's go in," he said, taking my hand.

A very surly looking bouncer stopped us, just on the other side of a white picket fence. "I.D.'s," he grumbled. Evan handed him his. I tried the same routine that we pulled on the waiter. "No I.D., no entry." I was certainly not getting past this guy. I looked to Evan for guidance. He shrugged his shoulders and went inside.

I stood there for what felt like an eternity. The bouncer just stood stoic, arms crossed, staring at me. I turned and backtracked to the hotel. I didn't cry until I got back into the room. I sat on the edge of the bed and sobbed. The sleep bed. Luckily, Evan left the minibar key in the room. I downed two little bottles of Gordon's and passed out.

Sometime before dawn, Evan staggered back into the room. He stripped down to his briefs and crawled into bed. He started kissing me and told me he loved me. I had longed to hear those words, just not at that moment. And then it was his turn to cry. He confessed that he met a gay couple on the island and went back to their house and slept with them. He then said that he had a problem with drugs and alcohol and that he would get help upon our return. I suspected that he had a problem, but I didn't want to see it. I made him sleep in the sex bed.

In the morning, we didn't speak a word to one another. For the eight-hour car ride home, we didn't say a word. We didn't touch. The car was full of tension and Depeche Mode. When we arrived at my house, I grabbed my backpack and rumpled up suit from the backseat and slammed the door. I still didn't say a word to him. That was the last time I ever saw Evan.

Have a Nice Life
(Memory #3)

My mother was of the school of thought that her parenting obligations ended the moment I turned 18 and graduated from high school. My father was nonexistent. After their divorce, I saw very little of him. I was ok with that as he was never really present in my life. I often felt that they should never have had me. They were both 20 when I was born. After my arrival, my mother wanted to be a mom and my father did not want to be a dad. That's where their problems began.

From the time I admitted to myself that I was gay, I had a crush on Nate, a fellow classmate of mine. He was captain of the football team, honor roll student, extremely popular amongst our class and was hung like a mule. Thank you gym class showers for that one. He was also charming and stunningly handsome. Chocolate brown eyes, puppy dog smile, jet-black hair and slightly olive skin. I loved whatever class I had with him. I was disappointed when he took Spanish and I took French, one less opportunity to be together.

I would often leave him notes in his locker to meet me after school. Somehow he always obliged. Maybe he took pity on me. Either way, I was fine with it. We would talk of nothing really, school gossip and the like. He even invited me over to watch *The Blues Brothers*. I sat awkwardly in his living room with his parents as we watched the movie.

I couldn't tell if he was gay. He had a girlfriend, but he

was always so kind and gentle with me. I took it as hope that he would return my affections. I decided to come out to him and ask him on a date. Why? I have no idea. I had read stories of such situations ending badly. Even in death sometimes. I didn't think Nate was that cruel. I mean, he wouldn't jeopardize his full scholarship to the UW.

Nate,

I've wanted to tell you this for a long time, and you probably already suspect it, but I have the biggest crush on you. I hope that you feel the same.

Kyle

I slipped the note into his locker and silently said a prayer that this would work out the way I wanted it to. After the last class of the day, I looked for Nate. He was nowhere to be found, which was weird as we had an unspoken daily date. I shrugged it off and went home.

"Kyle! Nate is here to see you," my mom called from the kitchen. Nate entered my bedroom, looking like someone just backed over his dog. He closed my bedroom door and sat on the edge of the bed. I closed my biology textbook and waited for him to speak.

"I, uh," he stammered. "I got your letter."

"Ok," I said.

"Listen. You're great. You really are. I'm just not gay." My lower lip started to tremble and tears welled up in my eyes. "We can still be friends." He stood up and left as quickly as he came. That's when the tears flowed. I was so embarrassed. Mortified really. Not only were my affections not returned, but also I outted myself to him. I doubted he would tell anyone out of embarrassment, but still.

"Are you gay?" Mom asked, standing in my doorway, tears in her eyes.

"You know the answer to that," I said. She started crying.

"What will the neighbors think?" This was an odd question as we weren't friendly with any of our neighbors. Despite living in a small town, we weren't exactly the casserole swapping, swing by for a drink or a game of cards kind of neighbors.

"That I'm Kyle," I said. It was the best I could come up with in that moment. She left and I shut the door as quickly as I could. I sat on the floor opposite my stereo and put Nina Simone in the disc player. Nina's pain, while vastly different from mine, was pain and it was comforting. I cried until I passed out, waking up some time in the night to turn off the CD player, saying goodnight to Nina.

After graduation, I steered clear of my mom. She tried to blame my being gay on my father and the lack of his presence. I told her that was too easy. Not that I wanted to defend him, but it was true. I knew it wasn't his "fault." The summer went by quickly as I had Evan to occupy my time.

When it came time to begin my studies at UW-Milwaukee, she and my stepfather packed up the van and drove the two and a half hours to campus. I got checked in, found my room and carted my belongings to it. When everything was done, Mom turned to me and said: "Have a nice life."

Failure to Launch
(Memory #4)

The Architecture Building was a sleek, slender building made from glass rectangles, stainless steel doors and window frames, white walls and grey tiled floors. I pulled open the door on the East Hartford Avenue side of the building and slowly walked the steel stairs to the second floor. It was the same trip I had made a short two years ago when I toured the college and met with my academic advisor, Jean. I was summoned to her office under much different circumstances this time.

Student work lined the main hallway. *Arch 380 Drawing in Architecture* pieces were on display. I glanced at each piece, knowing that mine wouldn't be hanging next to those. I stopped outside Jean's door, holding off going in for as long as I could.

Two years. That's all it took going from hopeful architecture student to failure. Everything I had started while at UWM was a failure. I joined the student orchestra as bassist. We were playing Dvorak's Symphony No. 8. I never made it to the concert. I was passionate about my Urban Planning course, yet I didn't show up for the final. I longed to continue my French studies but didn't attend the lectures or conversation group meetings.

I stayed in bed, missing Evan. At first, friends tried to pull me out of my funk. They'd force me to join them for late night dinners at the Palm Garden in the dormitory complex. Breaded chicken sandwiches and fries, washed down with a Diet Coke, did nothing to revive the spark in me. Green Day played above us on the stereo.

I made plans to move into an apartment with Ruth, an oboist whom I met in the orchestra. She wanted to live off campus and I was being forced out of the dorms so it worked out well. Well, save for the fact I had no money and no job. It was all on borrowed time.

I could see the outline of Jean through the frosted glass door to her office. I still couldn't go in. Going in would make it official. I wasn't ready for that. I had even tried to blame my absenteeism on my grandfather's death. He wasn't dead and the school wanted proof. That wasn't happening.

I walked my belongings over to the new apartment. My oversized print of Monet's Water Lilies I bought in France on a class trip, suitcases with my clothing. And my Macintosh Performa computer, purchased with my new American Express card, which I had no idea how I was able to get.

My friends would still be around. The apartment was so close to campus they could come over any time they wished. They didn't though. They were busy with their studies and after school activities. This isolated me further, sending me deeper into depression.

I sighed and opened the office door. Jean forced half a smile.

"Kyle, please sit down." I obeyed. "Kyle," she continued, taking off her glasses and setting them on a pile of manila folders. "This is not easy, but you have to understand there is no other course of action at this point."

"There's nothing that can be done?" One last plea.

"I'm afraid not. You are officially removed from the School of Architecture and Urban Planning. You are eligible to reenter the program after one year." That seemed like a lifetime away. My pride wanted to keep me enrolled. Deep in the pit of me, I knew Architecture was not for me. She handed me a piece of paper signed by the dean. I didn't read it.

"Kyle, I'm so sorry it's come to this. We saw such promise in you. Your enthusiasm and your intellect would have been perfect for the field of Architecture." It all seemed so irreparable.

"Can't I be placed on probation or something?"

"Kyle. You were on probation this past school year. You've made no attempts to make up the lost coursework. Furthermore, you didn't even show up to a single class this past semester alone. That hardly proves your dedication to turning this around." She was right. I didn't have an argument to stand on. I took the piece of paper and left her office without saying goodbye.

Grand Theft Auto
(Memory #5)

"She's a thing of beauty, isn't she?" asked the salesman. I smiled as I looked up at him. He was in his 50s, balding, thick salt and pepper mustache and his belly hung over his belt. He tapped the hood of the car.

"Yes, she is," I replied, staring at the shiny Mercedes-Benz 190E with jet-black metallic paint, perfect black leather interior, burl wood on the console, dash and doors. I loved the solid thud it made when closing the doors. I ran my hand across the tinted glass moonroof.

"You want to take her for a test drive?" I nodded and got into the driver's seat. The salesman got in next to me. He smelled like Polo cologne. It reminded me of my high school principal who also wore it. You could always tell if he had been where you were by the wake of cologne that trailed behind him.

The car drove like a dream. I kept staring at the logo on the steering wheel. I didn't go too far as I really didn't know my way around Milwaukee. I knew the campus area and down Downer and Prospect Avenues to downtown, but that was it. Back at the dealership, I thanked the salesman and headed out to the bus stop. I laughed at the fact I had taken public transportation to test drive a luxury car.

Back at my apartment, all I could think of was the car. How cool I would look driving it, how envious my friends would be of it and all the places that I could go. I felt isolated, now that I was longer enrolled in college and was tethered to the bus system. I let out a sigh and thought: I don't even have a job, much less the money for a car. I opened the kitchen cabinet next to the sink. One lone packet of ramen. I took it out and poured hot water over it.

The next morning, the phone rang. "Hello?" I said, answering the call.

"Kyle? This is Gerald, from the dealership."

"Oh, yes," I said, rubbing my eyes. "What can I do for you?"

"I wanted to follow up with you about the Mercedes we have here."

"It's a great car. Really, it is. It's just out of my price range."

"Well, that's also why I am calling. What if we take two thousand off? Nineteen thousand? You will not find this car at that price anywhere else." It was true. I had done my research.

"Let me think about it." I thanked him and hung up the phone and crawled back in bed. I was suffering from a severe case of depression. I thought the car was the answer. It would make me feel better about myself, allow me the freedom to leave Milwaukee whenever I wanted and I had always dreamt about owning car like that. I fell back asleep, daydreaming about pulling into Mineral Point in my new Mercedes.

I woke up around 6 P.M. and stayed in bed. I looked at my checkbook balance. I had enough money for one more trip to the grocery store. I thought about looking for a job and that just made me more depressed. I knew I should have been in college with my classmates. The types of jobs I could get without a college degree were pretty much limited to retail and food service. There was no way I was going to do that.

I stewed over the car for a week. In my head, all signs were pointing to yes. But, where was I going to get money for it? I came up with a plan. I would buy the car with a check and then I would contact my grandparents and ask them for the money, telling them that I had to cover the check. I knew if I asked them for a loan outright, they would say no. But, how could they say no in my hour of need?

I took the bus back to the dealership. I found Gerald sitting in a cubical in the back, eating a sandwich from KFC. "Kyle!" he said, standing up to shake my hand. I could feel the oil on my hand and wiped it discreetly on my pants.

"I think I'm ready to buy her," I said, taking out my checkbook.

"Great! Let's get the paperwork started." I sat down across from him. He wrapped up what was left of his sandwich and placed it to the side. He took out a stack of papers from the desk drawer and began writing. I told him a story that this was a late graduation gift from my grandparents and that they had loaned me the money.

Once the title transfer paperwork was complete, I showed proof of insurance and handed him the check and in return got the keys. It all happened so quickly. I ran my hand across the glossy silver Mercedes logo and smiled.

"Great doing business with you, Kyle!" Gerald said. "Take care of that little gem."

"Oh, I will!" I got in the car and left the lot. Back at my apartment, I threw some clothes in a bag and then headed towards Mineral Point. I was going to surprise Melissa by showing up at her house. For the two and a half hours I drove, the guilt was piled on. What if my grandparents refused me the money? What then? I felt like I was in the opening scenes of *Psycho*. I turned on the radio to drown out my thoughts.

I honked as I pulled up next to Melissa's house. She came out with a confused look on her face and a dishtowel in her hands.

"Kyle?" she asked as I exited the car, curious what I was doing unannounced at her house and in a Mercedes no less.

"Do you like it? I just bought it."

"Wow," she said.

"Want to go for a ride?" She nodded and closed her front door. "How did you pay for this?" she said she ran her hand along the dash.

"I didn't. I'm going to get the money from my grandparents." I told her of my plan and she just shook her head.

"Oh, Kyle. You really did it this time." I asked if I

could stay over and she said yes. That night, in the guest room, I could see the car from my bed, shrouded in moonlight. A knot in my stomach was growing tighter. Melissa was right. This was wrong. I had no idea how I was going to get myself out of this.

During the car ride back to Milwaukee, I prepared my speech in my head to deliver to my grandparents. I couldn't fathom having that conversation face-to-face so I decided to wait until I was back in my apartment.

The conversation did not go as I had schemed. My grandfather was livid with me. He told me to not drive the car again and wait until I heard back from him. I crawled back in bed after hanging up the phone. What had I done?

The next day the phone rang. I didn't have caller I.D. and assumed it was my grandfather, calling me back to tell me he had changed his mind and would cover the money.

"Kyle?" said a familiar voice. "You little shit. Do you really think you can get away with this?" It was Gerald. Obviously my check did not clear. I didn't know what to say. Thankfully, Gerald had plenty to say. "You need to get that car back here this second you little fucker. Do you know what this is? This is Grand Theft Auto, a felony conviction. Do you want that?" I could almost feel his spit and rage through the phone. I felt like I was going to faint.

I called my grandfather immediately after. He told me that his lawyer in Madison would be handling this for me and that said lawyer would be calling me shortly for the details. He then told me how disappointed he was in me, that he had hoped great things would come from my life. I hung up the phone and sobbed.

As he foretold, the lawyer called me and collected all the necessary information. He called me back an hour later to tell me that a deal had been struck. I was to return the car that day and the dealership would not press charges. My grandfather would pay them an unsaid amount in damages and I would have to surrender my checkbook, credit cards and file for bankruptcy. I agreed.

I put the title and all paperwork neatly in the glove compartment and headed towards the dealership. I stopped a block before the lot to see if I could spot Gerald or anyone else. When the coast was clear, I drove the car onto the lot, parked it, shut it off and ran for the bus stop. As luck would have it, there was a bus waiting. I jumped on and slouched down in a seat. I could see Gerald come running out of the dealership looking around for me.

Once the dealership was out of sight, I sat back up and started to cry. It was hardly my finest hour.

Westward
(Memory #6)

I began chatting with Eddie as my time in Milwaukee was coming to a head. I knew my days were numbered before I was going to be kicked out of my apartment. I didn't share this with Eddie. The distraction from it all was much needed.

Eddie was studying French at the University of Arizona at Tucson. He was shorter than me, was really skinny, and had curly blond hair and the cutest face. And he was into me. Miracle of miracles. He said he lived alone in a one-bedroom apartment and that his sister was also living in town. He said they were very close, seeing one another almost daily. She was studying Philosophy.

"I have an idea," said Eddie, not saying hello as I picked up the phone.

"Tell me."

"I have money left over from my scholarships. Let me buy you a ticket to come meet me. I have midterms right now, but it would be a nice distraction. What do you say?"

"You're sweet. You really are. But, I'm broke."

"Don't worry about it! I will buy the ticket and you'll stay with me. I will pick you up from the airport and drop you off. And I'm a great cook!"

"I don't want to be a charity case."

"You wouldn't be! I want to do this! Believe me. It's hard enough to find someone who I click with. Especially the way we do. *S'il vous plaît?*" He knew I took French in high school.

"Ok," I said, wondering how I would pay my way to the airport. Yeah, I was *that* broke. I combed the apartment and scraped up enough money for bus fare. The next day, he emailed me that the ticket had been purchased. I was flying out the following day.

The bus dropped me off at General Mitchell Airport. The air was biting and sharp. I ran inside to escape the cold. Arizona would be a great chance to warm up. And maybe, being out of my normal surroundings, I would figure out what I was going to do. I got my ticket and boarded the plane.

"Kyle?" he said as I exited the gate in Tucson.

"Eddie?" I returned the question. He looked great. He hugged me. He came up to my chin.

"It's so great to meet you! How was the flight?"

"It was great. Thank you again for doing this. You really didn't have to."

"Nonsense. I wanted to. C'mon, my truck is this way." Did I hear that right? A truck? Not what I pictured him driving. But, he did, a bright red Toyota truck that sat two people. I put my suitcase in the back and climbed in, folding my winter coat over my lap. Hours earlier, I was freezing. Now I had the

31

window down and the warm night air blowing across me.

Eddie lived on the second floor of a duplex in a complex with dozens of identical units. Each building was made of soft orange stucco with dark orange tiled roofs. We climbed the outdoor staircase to his apartment.

"Sorry, it's not much."

"Don't sweat it!" I said, entering his living room. He wasn't joking. He had no artwork on the walls, a futon and a T.V. in the living room, a retro looking stainless steel and Formica table and chairs in the kitchen, and a bed with one nightstand in the bedroom. It really was sparsely decorated. I was hoping to study framed photos, anything that would give me deeper access to who he was.

"Can I offer you something to drink? I have beer, wine and water."

"I'll have a glass of wine." He took a plastic cup with a local bar's logo on it from the cupboard and poured me a glass of pinot noir. I would definitely have to upgrade this guy's place if we dated, I thought. Wine in a plastic cup? *Tsk tsk.*

He grabbed a beer and sat down next to me on the futon. He was sitting very close to me. This was a good sign. He gently caressed my arm as he drank his beer. He was so adorable. I started to get hard. I wondered how we would make this relationship work with the distance. Then again, I knew that my time in Milwaukee had all but expired. Did I want to move to

Arizona? I would miss grass and snow.

Eddie leaned in and kissed me. I could taste the beer on his lips. I wondered if he could taste the wine on mine. I ran my hands through his golden curls and he gently ran his thumb down my cheeks. I could hear a semi shifting gears somewhere on the highway.

"Let's go in the bedroom," he said, standing up and dragging me with.

He pulled back the comforter and turned off the lamp and turned on the oscillating fan in the corner of the room. That was good, I thought, as I required white noise in order to fall asleep.

After sex, Eddie fell asleep with this head on my chest. Normally, I can't sleep if someone is touching me, but I was exhausted from the trip and fell asleep not long after he did.

In the morning, I woke after he did. I pulled on my clothes and went into the kitchen where I found a hot cup of coffee waiting for me and Eddie at the stove making pancakes.

"Good morning," I said as I entered.

"Good morning." We kissed and I sat at the table. "I don't know how you take your coffee, so there's sugar there and milk in the fridge."

"Black is fine. Thank you for making me breakfast." He smiled at me and returned to his cooking. After we ate, we showered together and got dressed. He was working part time at a café and said I could come and hang out there, he would comp me whatever I wanted and I could wander around the area if I got bored.

Seated at an outdoor table, under a giant yellow umbrella I pulled out *Dangerous Liaisons*, which I was reading. Eddie informed me he read it in the original French. Of course he did, I thought. He brought me a Diet Coke with lemon and for the next few hours I quietly read my book. I would look up every so often to see him with customers. He would look at me and smile.

After his shift, we went and saw *The English Patient* and had dinner at a tiny Greek diner. After, we returned to his apartment and had sex again. Something was different this time. It lacked the intensity of the first time. But, it was still very natural and comforting to be with him.

In the morning, I woke before he did. Lying sideways, I stared at him, watching him sleep. He was becoming more beautiful to me. He looked so innocent and gentle as he slept. If he asked me to move to Arizona, I'd say yes, I thought.

When he woke, he didn't have that grin that I was quickly getting used to. We showered separately and he barely said a word to me as we drove back to the airport. What had I done? Things were going so well! I couldn't figure it out.

Eddie pulled the truck over at the terminal. I could see it on his face. This was over. "Kyle," he started. "I had a great time with you. I really did. You're awesome. I just don't think this is going to work out."

"Why?" I asked, but I knew the answer.

"You have no money, no job, and no college education. What are you going to do with your life?"

I grabbed my bag and l exited the truck. I didn't look back. Once on board the plane, I started to cry. The flight attendant asked me if I was ok. I asked if I could have a bottle of vodka. She brought me three.

Best Laid Plans
(Memory #7)

I started crying as I closed the door to my father's truck.
He finished securing a bungee cord across the back.
Everything I owned was under that blue tarp, my books,
my clothes, a couple random pieces of furniture that I
collected from people moving out of the dorms and no
longer needing them, and my computer. I could see my
roommate Ruth standing in our living room window.
She didn't wave, just stood there motionless. It had
been a good four months since I had paid rent and she
was (rightfully) pissed at me and eventually evicted me.
Such an opposite end to the way our friendship began.

My dad got in the truck and started it up. He didn't say
a word. I turned my head away from him to hide my
tears, but it was obvious I was crying. He also made no
judgments. That was nice. There was a benefit to him
not taking any sort of interest in my life.

I thought of my friends back at UW-Milwaukee as the
city skyline drew smaller in the rear view mirror. I had
such hopes of becoming the next great architect.
Pushing ecological design to the mainstream and taking
its aesthetic from hippie commune to high art. I had
been kicked out of the School of Architecture two years
after graduating from high school. For the time
following, I floated from job to job to job. Finally,
something in me gave up.

Milwaukee was out of view. Dad and I continued to
ride in silence. I was moving back in with my mother
and stepfather. I was dreading their lectures and

opinions on what I should be doing with my life. What was I going to do? Where was I going to work? How was I going to pay for a car? How would I afford an apartment on my own? Would I return to college? What would I major in? How would I pay for it? I sighed as we pulled into Madison. Dad asked if I was hungry. We stopped at Subway and got lunch. Neither of us said anything while we ate.

There were a few good memories from that short time. I forced myself to think back on them. There was the first time I got drunk. I had made friends with several music majors and they invited me out with them. We went to this sports bar near campus and I got wasted doing "blow job" shots. Then, I climbed into a container housing salt to spread on the sidewalk. I would throw open the lid as people walked by, screaming at them to get away from my house, why were they trying to take my house? I woke up the next morning on the lawn of the Lutheran church next to campus. Apparently, before passing out, I was exclaiming that I was drunk at God's house.

There was the time when Sally and I got drunk and decided to t.p. the school forest. We failed miserably, learning years later that you need to hold one end of the toilet paper while throwing it and unraveling it as it went. We just threw whole rolls in the air that did nothing but return to us intact.

And there were boyfriends. Mainly Andrew. Oh, Andrew. I met him at the bank that I got a job at as someone's personal assistant. He was my age, worked in Human Resources and was beautiful, with pale skin, dotted with freckles, dark brown hair and soulful eyes. I was in the bathtub when I decided that I was

going to ask him out. I called him up and he actually
said yes. We dated for three months and then things
began to fizzle. He wanted to go out to gay clubs more
than he wanted to be with me. After having gone to the
clubs a handful of times, only to be met with rejection, I
avoided going at all costs. He eventually dumped
me. Three months was my longest relationship.

What was I going to do? No job, no money, no college
education and living with my mother. I shuddered. By
the time we arrived back in Mineral Point, I had
finished draining myself of tears. The truck turned
down Fountain Street and my mom's house slowly
came into view. There she was, standing just outside
the front door with her hands on her hips and a scowl
on her face.

"Oh, fuck," I said.

Family Dinner

"It's so good to see you," said Grandma, lighting a cigarette at her kitchen table. Sugar-free candies scattered across stacks of old newspapers. She flicked her ashes into an empty Diet Pepsi bottle. I could see several butts in the bottom, in a syrupy brown liquid. I pray I don't accidentally drink from that, I thought.

"It's great to see you, too! What's new?"

"Nothing really. Lois passed away. I think I emailed you that though." She did. "They're building a new gas station up on the highway." I saw that. "Say, what are your plans for dinner?"

"I don't have any."

"Oh, ok. I didn't know if you were meeting up with one of your friends." I shook my head. I forgot what it was like to be around smokers. Since passing the no smoking law in New York, I only encountered smokers briefly on the street as I raced to get around them.

Grandma pulled her cellphone off the holster on her belt and dialed a number. A few seconds later, her call was answered. "How we doing?" she asked, taking another drag from her cigarette. "Guess who I'm sitting with? Yup. What are you and Bonnie doing for dinner? Oh, ok. You want to head over to Country Kitchen in Dodgeville?" She firmed up plans and ended the call. "That was your dad. I thought it would be nice if we all went to dinner."

"It would," I said because I knew it was the right thing

to say. It's not that I didn't want to have dinner with my father and his wife. It was that I had no real connection to him. He had more in common with my younger brother who also liked to hunt, fish and work on cars. Dad never came to my recitals, concerts or awards dinners. He came home from his job as a welder and barely spoke a word to me. Now, we really only speak on birthdays and Christmas.

Grandma and I climbed up into her truck, a massive, brand new Ford truck. She had long since sold off all the cattle and fields of the family farm, but she was so used to driving a pickup that she continued to buy them. I asked her to crack the window a little as she lit another cigarette.

We, of course, were late. Punctuality rests in the highest of esteem with me. If you're going to show up to something, at least be on time. Inside, I saw my dad, his wife, my mom, her husband, my brother and his wife all seated at the table. I said hello to everyone and took a seat at the end of the table. Grandma sat next to me. "You surprised to see everyone? I called your brother and your mom when you were in the bathroom."

"Very surprised," I said.

Our waitress approached us with two menus. "I think we'll all have the buffet," Grandma announced. I watched as everyone flopped their menus down on the table. "This way, everyone gets a little bit of everything." Her logic defied me. I mean, for the same price, I could get exactly what I wanted off the menu and not have to eat from that trough. Buffets skeeved me out; all that food, sitting out forever under heat

lamps, food dropping into the neighboring dish, people
using their dirty hands, sneezing on the sneeze guard.

Each of us stood up, single file and grabbed a
plate. When it was my turn, I looked over the selection
and tried to find the least offensive offering. I grabbed
a couple pieces of chicken fingers and fries with a
greasy pair of tongs. I scooped steamed corn onto my
plate as well as a scoop of cornbread stuffing. Random,
I thought. Grandma had an indiscernible pile of food
on her plate.

My brother, Benjamin, was telling the table about a
recent fishing trip he had been on in Canada. His wife,
Anne, a perky tax accountant who worked in Madison,
pressed me for details about life in New York. While I
was in their wedding, I didn't really know her all that
well. I knew she was sweet and complimented my
brother perfectly. That's it.

"Isn't this good?" said Grandma, taking a bite of a
brownish, greyish piece of meat. I looked at Anne and
we both smiled, neither of us really eating our food.

It was odd yet natural to have both my parents and their
new partners at the dinner together. They had been
unhappy together but found happiness with someone
else. Who was I to judge? My dad looked so much
older from the last time I saw him. I wondered if that
was my fate. I thought I would stop in Madison and get
some anti-aging products.

After dinner, Grandma paid as I gave everyone a hug
and told them how great it was to see them again. In a
way it was. They were familiar strangers. Back in the
truck, Grandma handed me a hundred-dollar bill.

"What's this for?" I said, taking it in my hand but not pocketing it yet.

"Your mom told me about your job." I dropped my hand to the seat. Of course she did.

Movin' On Up!
(Memory #8)

Living with my mother again was punishment enough. At every opportunity, she reminded me that I was 21 years old and living back at home. She taunted me with the fact that my classmates were well into their college careers and soon would be graduating. Some even going on to graduate school while I didn't even have an Associate's degree. Thanks, Mom.

My stepfather retired from the army after twenty years of service. He ran the house like the barracks. Each day of the week had its own routine: grocery shopping on Monday, laundry on Tuesday, Wednesday was yard work and so on. All the items in the pantry were placed labels facing out. The spice cabinet was alphabetical. Their bed linens were made with crisp hospital corners.

I kept to myself, in my room, as much as I could. I had taken a job at Walmart, in the shoe department. That was pretty much the lowest point of my existence. The upside was that none of my peers shopped for shoes at Walmart and the department was stuck way in the back corner of the store, easily avoided.

My mother would transport me to and from work. Sometimes, I would have to wait for her in the snack bar. I stared at hotdogs rolling back and forth. I asked myself why? What's next? A cheesy crust had formed on the spout of the nacho cheese dispenser. I wanted to cry, but couldn't. Giant, salted pretzels turned on a rack, under a heat lamp.

I had my computer with me. The one expensive possession I owned, an Apple Performa 575. I opened an Internet account with a local provider and was reconnected to my Milwaukee friends. Little had changed. My absence wasn't felt, it seemed.

I sat in front of my stereo and put Rachmaninoff Piano Concerto No. 2 into the CD player. I rested my head on my hands and sighed, still not able to cry. I was throwing a blowout pity party for myself. And like many such parties, I had no guests.

Listening to the concerto, I was reminded of how in high school, I passionately wanted to be a concert pianist. I was good, too. I was even offered a scholarship to UW-Platteville to study piano. I declined. I wish I hadn't. If I couldn't go to Juilliard (and I wasn't *that* good), I didn't want it.

"Kyle! Phone!" Mom shouted from the kitchen. I picked up the headset in my room.

"Hello?"

"Kyle, it's your grandma. I wanted to let you know that we have an apartment vacant downtown if you want it. We'll give you a break on the rent too, only $300 a month."

I was making money now and the prospect of living anywhere where my parents weren't was good enough for me. "Great! Where is the place?"

"It's on High Street. Can you meet me there in an hour?" I got the details and put my shoes on. My mom, as she did every time I received a phone call, asked who it was and what was wanted. I could see, although she'd never say anything, she was relieved at the idea of me moving out. Again.

The new place was about a fifteen-minute walk from my mom's. I felt like I was walking on air the whole way there. I crossed the highway and made my way down to High Street. The apartment was in a building at the top of the street, Mineral Point's main street. There were two apartments above it. The vacant unit was in back, an exposed basement studio apartment. I knocked on the door.

"Come in, Kyle," my grandma said. I knew she was in there. I could see her Cadillac parked out front. No one else in Mineral Point drove such a nice vehicle. I pushed the door open to find a shell of a space. No carpeting, walls in dire need of painting and a kitchen that consisted of a sink, a broken looking fridge and a counter with homemade cabinets. "It's not much is it?"

"Well, a coat of paint and it will be fine," I said, beyond desperate to move out on my own.

"You don't mind painting it?"

"No," I said.

"Ok. Your grandfather and I will pay for the paint. Just let us know which color." It was settled. The following week they'd buy the paint and as soon as I had completed my work, I could move in. The place was a total dump, but I couldn't have been happier. I kind of looked forward to the project of fixing it up.

I leisurely walked back home. As I was telling my mom the good news, the phone rang. It was my grandmother.

"Listen dear, I spoke with your grandfather and we just can't let you live like that. There is some money set aside for repairs on the building, so we are going to remodel it for you. It won't be ready for a couple of months, but it will be brand new. And we'll keep the rent at $300." My grandfather was a big shot local real estate agent. He managed the building for someone. I was bummed I would have to wait, but relished in the idea of having a brand new place. If I couldn't drive a brand new car, at least I could live well.

The next two months dragged on. Every so often, I would stop by the new place to see the progress. There was new wiring, drywall, cabinets, appliances, bathtub, toilet, sink and vanity, heating units. Soon, a fresh coat of paint called "rice paper" was applied, new golden oak trim framed all edges and brown berber carpet was set.

"Here are the keys," Grandma said. I took them with a huge sense of relief, a step in the right direction. I looked around the space and thought about where I would put things. For the short term, I had an inflatable mattress that I used. Eventually, I bought a black metal-framed futon that would serve as my sofa and bed. I found an old mid-century modern chair at a yard sale and my father and his wife donated a table and chairs to me when they bought a new set. My apartment had come together.

For the next four months, I settled in quite

comfortably. I had phone service established and set up my computer and modem. I cooked my own meals and every night I would curl up in my new chair and watch *Mystery Science Theatre 3000*. I even bought a plant. I still needed a car, but one out of two wasn't bad.

I had my old piano moved from my parents to the new place. I would play Bach and Beethoven at least once a day.

But, with all of this newness and starting over, I couldn't mask my loneliness. I would still bump into classmates and hear stories of how everyone's lives were moving forward. I wasn't exactly standing still, but I didn't feel like I was making progress. Kind of moving diagonally. At a snail's pace.

I sat down at my kitchen table to feast on raspberry chicken that I made, having pulled the recipe out of my head. The phone rang. It was my mother.

"I have some good news for you," she said. She never had good news.

"What's that?" I said, cutting into my chicken.

"There was a posting on the job board at work that I think you'd like." Mom worked at Roads' End (as we will call them here, a prominent clothing catalog based in Dodgeville, a town over from Mineral Point).

"What is it?" I asked, taking a bite. Not bad, I thought.

"It's for a CAD operator."

"I have no CAD experience."

"They will train you. It's a three-week course. It's for the business-to-business group. You would be digitizing corporate logos that get embroidered onto stuff."

"Cool." It sounded way better than the shoe department. "What do I need to do?"

"Do you have a pen? I am going to give you an email address to send your resume to." I jotted down the info.

"Thank you," I said and hung up the phone.

After dinner, I washed the dishes (a dishwasher didn't come with the new place, unfortunately) and thought about what I would say in my email. I didn't exactly have a lot of experience on my resume, but had one nonetheless.

Sent. I sat back in my chair and checked my email. Nothing. I scanned the personals for the area. Not one. Looked at a few in Madison and decided against writing anyone. I mean, I didn't have a car even to go on a date, much less land a man.

I shut down my computer, poured a glass of Bombay Blue Sapphire and sat in the big windowsill facing High Street. I watched the cars go up and down the hill, just as I had done with my friends in high school. There I was, still in Mineral Point. Hardly where I thought my life would be.

Loose Threads
(Memory #9)

"See you Monday! Again, congratulations." I hung up the phone and sighed. I got the job. I was now a CAD Designer at Roads' End. No more shoe department. I thought of Al Bundy on *Married with Children* and laughed. A fate avoided.

In my excitement and haste, I realized that I wouldn't be giving Walmart the standard two weeks notice. There was a CAD training session starting on Monday and I didn't want to wait until another one would get scheduled. I called my manager, who was sympathetic, knowing that it was a way better opportunity and agreed to let me out early.

I took a frozen pizza out and put it in the oven and called my mom. "I got the job!" I said and thanked her. It also helped, I'm sure, that she worked over in the call center at Roads' End. I took the pizza out of the oven and turned on the modem. No emails. I idly surfed the Internet while eating my dinner. Things were looking up.

Roads' End occupied a sprawling campus on the north side of Dodgeville, fenced in on three sides by cornfields. My mom dropped me off at Building 6 and headed over to her work at Building 1. The building had just been built to accommodate the growing business-to-business program. I made my way to reception and got checked in and was shown to a conference room with multiple computer stations set up.

I was the first to arrive. I doodled in my notebook while I waited. I noticed that each station had a thread book containing the various embroidery thread color options. I began playing with them, creating unique color combinations. A girl with a permed mullet and four-inch high bangs came in and sat at the station next to mine.

"How's it going?" she asked with a heavy lisp.

"Good. How are you?"

"Good. I'm Tina."

"Kyle," I said, shaking her hand. It was like the first day of school, a more professional first day of school where I got paid to show up. Soon, the other six people showed up and we began. We were shown how to take customers' logos, scan them into the computer and then meticulously digitize them so the multi-head embroidery machines could read the files and stitch them. We were thread alchemists, converting a flat jpeg file into a multidimensional piece of embroidery. I fell in love with embroidery. It wouldn't be until more than a decade later that I would start my own embroidery business, but I knew I loved it.

On the weekends, I would walk down to the library and check out books on sewing and design. While I was in Milwaukee, someone on my floor in the dorms had rented *Unzipped,* the Isaac Mizrahi documentary about putting together a runway collection. I was mesmerized by this world of beautiful colors, fabrics, materials and textures and crazy personalities. I saw a lot of myself in Isaac. He struggled with his weight, loved old

Technicolor movies, and played the piano. A seed had been planted.

For Christmas, my mom asked me what I wanted. It was easy: a sewing machine. I began buying Vogue patterns and recreated the garments the best I could, teaching myself as I went. I am a quick learner and sewing came natural to me. I could look at a set of patterns, not unlike a set of blueprints, and quickly see the final product. Plus, I loved the tactile nature of creating something from a pile of raw materials. At first, I didn't give away the garments I made. They hung quietly on the garment rack next to my kitchen.

I would lose all concept of time the moment I sat behind the machine and put my foot on the pedal. Most weekends, I would sew all day Saturday, pausing only to catch a new episode of *Mystery Science Theater 3000*. For my birthday, I got an adjustable dress form. Piles of fabric lined the windowsill by my dining table, which had permanently become my sewing station. A plastic bin full of bobbins of thread sat on top of a stack of sheet music on the piano. It would not be out of the ordinary for people to pick stray threads off my clothes. For the first time in a long time, I was happy.

A Friend of a Friend
(Memory #10)

I waited as patiently as I could, at my apartment for
Harry. I had met him online, chatted for a few weeks
and decided to meet. He had been visiting his family in
Dubuque, Iowa for the weekend and was traveling
through Mineral Point, on his way back to
Madison. He was very tall, lanky, and pale skinned
with dark hair. He looked very bohemian in his photos,
like he shopped at thrift stores, in a cool way.

There was a knock at the door. It was Harry. I opened
it and was met with a smile and a bouquet of
roses. "Thank you!" I said. He pulled me in for a
hug. Forward, I thought, but harmless, just the same.

"Kyle, it's so great to meet you!"

"You too. Come in," I offered. He took off his long
plaid wool overcoat and handed it to me. "Please, sit
down," I motioned towards the living "room." He sat
on the floor near the stereo, which I thought was odd,
but whatever. I hung his coat on the back of a kitchen
chair and joined him on the floor. Miles Davis' *Kind of
Blue* was playing in the CD player. A music lover, he
was drawn to the stereo like he had come in from the
cold and found a crackling fire.

"This is a great CD."

"Yeah, it's one of my favorites." We sat in awkward
silence. He was smiling and staring at me. Suddenly, I
thought, maybe meeting at my place wasn't such a good

idea.

"Can I kiss you?" he asked.

"Yes," I said. He leaned in and took my head sweetly and gently in his hands and kissed me. He was a very good kisser. He pulled me closer and soon I was sitting on his lap, arms wrapped around one another, Miles playing next to us.

Soon our clothes were off, the futon was flattened and the deed was done. He asked if he could spend the night as it was late and he didn't feel like driving. I agreed. Next to him, in the dark, I looked at the shadows the blinds created on the ceiling. I couldn't help but not feel a connection to Harry. I wanted to, but it just wasn't there. I wondered if he sensed it, too. I looked over and he was fast asleep.

I didn't sleep much that night. I wasn't used to sharing my bed. Most nights, I didn't even put the futon down, choosing to sleep on it sofa style. Leaning into the back of it was comforting like sleeping in the fetal position.

"Good morning," he said, playing with the hair on my stomach. I wished he weren't there. And then I felt awful for thinking that. I really wanted to get up, shower and wait for my ride to work by myself. "I'll give you a ride to work," he offered.

"No, it's ok. Thank you, though." I was currently carpooling with two women who worked in my department. I didn't feel like telling them why I didn't need a ride that Monday morning. His hand slid under the covers. I flinched and moved to the side. "Sorry, I really don't have time. We should get ready."

We showered quickly together and got dressed. He took my head in his hands again and kissed me. I really wanted to make the bed. I was looking at it out of the corner of my eye.

"My ride will be here soon."

"Ok. When can I see you again?" he asked, pouty face and all.

"Email me. My schedule's pretty open."

"Ok, bye!" He kissed my forehead and was gone. I quickly put the futon back up and tore off the linens and put them in a pile to launder when I got home. I could hear the girls honking out front. I hoped that they had not seen Harry leave.

For one reason or another, I didn't see Harry again. We exchanged emails every so often. As it would later turn out, almost immediately, he met and started dating a guy named Tim in Madison. I felt relieved. They wanted to invite me over to his house in Madison to meet everyone. I agreed to go. I mean, why not? Just because Harry and I didn't work out, doesn't mean I can't be friends with him. That and I was dying to be around other people. People not from (sorry for the expression) my neck of the woods.

Harry lived on the east side of Madison. I could navigate the west side with no problem. It was the point of entry for just about every Madison trip I made. I could sort of make my way around downtown, if school wasn't in session. All the students on the street made me feel nervous like they were judging me. Judging me for not knowing where I was going and for not being in college. East side, forget it. I printed maps and wrote out a turn-by-turn direction list.

All of the apartments looked the same to me, that late seventies/early eighties bland, soulless, style-less duplex. I found Harry's apartment easily. It was the one that sounded like a party. Oh, God, I thought. I hated crowds and certainly ones full of strangers.

"Kyle!" Harry exclaimed from across the room.

"Hi Harry," I said.

"Come here! I want you to meet Tim." He introduced us. Tim seemed much more of a match for Harry than I. Avoiding small talk, I wandered into the kitchen and poured myself a glass of wine into a red Solo cup. One more reason why we can't date, I said to myself and laughed.

"Hi, I'm Phaedra," said this girl my age with bright orange hair and large, sparkling eyes.

"Hi, I'm Kyle," I said, shaking her hand. "How do you know Harry?"

"I don't. I know Tim. I've known him since high school."

"Ah. What do you think of Harry?" I asked bluntly.

"I don't know. I can't put my finger on it," she said, closing her eyes slightly in a pensive gesture.

"Right?!" I exclaimed, taking a sip of wine. I followed

her out to the living where we continued our conversation. Turns out she was a bassist with the Madison Symphony Orchestra. I had played bass in high school and briefly in college. She was a huge fan of fashion and the Spice Girls, two big plusses with me. We exchanged contact information and vowed to be friends. Almost twenty years later, we still are.

The Rabbit
(Memory #11)

Living anywhere outside of an urban area requires a car, a bike at the very least. And given the winters in Wisconsin, I wasn't about to cycle my way around. I used my great-grandmother's car for a while as her eyesight was failing. That only lasted a few weeks and then it crapped out. I was left to bum rides off of people. It wasn't until a few months later, luck struck.

"Kyle," my mom said on the phone. "I think we found a car for you."

"Really?" I said, visions of carting myself around whenever I wanted filled my head. "Tell me more."

"It's a navy blue Volkswagen Rabbit, four doors, moonroof, and has a hatchback. Good shape, just a little rust around the fenders."

"How much?"

"$100."

"That's it?" I almost shouted into the phone. "How come? What's wrong with it?"

"Well, that's a funny story. Your stepfather heard of this guy selling the car for parts, as it wouldn't start any longer. He bought it, put a new battery in it and it works perfectly."

"Oh, my God! This is great!"

"There's only one problem." Of course there was. It couldn't be that easy. "It's a standard transmission. You're going to have to learn." I was so desperate to have my independence that I didn't care. My mom came and got me the next day for a driving lesson.

She and my stepfather, at the time, owned a sprawling farm just north of Dodgeville. They had close to 200 acres, a pond, a barn, a machine shed, and a pasture with horses. And there was a gravel loop that went from the driveway entrance up and around the machine shed and back. This was my training ground.

"Shit," I said, grinding the gears, trying to find second.

"Easy," Mom said. I flashed a look that said back off. With a deep breath, I found second gear. "I think you're ready to hit the road. Let me get my purse and my list and you can take me to Walmart."

Soon we were off on the highway. I had taken to driving stick quite naturally I thought; only minor grinds of the gears and a few jerky starts. We were flying down the highway. I opened the moonroof and turned on the radio.

"This is a pretty great car!" I said. Mom smiled. I couldn't wait to drop her off and head to Madison. I had felt so trapped in my studio apartment with no car. I could only walk down to the corner restaurant so many times.

"Now watch out. You're coming up to the stoplight." The *only* stoplight in the county. I pressed the clutch and downshifted with grace. Very smooth, I thought. I pictured James Bond driving his Aston Martin.

We waited for a few minutes at the stoplight. One right turn and Walmart was there. Green light. I pressed the clutch and moved the shifter into first. A thud shook the entire car. I could tell something was wrong as it suddenly felt as though the shifter was not connected to anything underneath. I pressed on the gas pedal but went nowhere. I tried again. Nothing. The car stalled. People were now driving around me, shaking their heads. In New York, I would have been honked at, but Wisconsin was more polite.

"The transmission is gone!" Mom said, stating the obvious.

"I know!"

"What are we doing to do?!" she screamed.

"Get out and push it!" I screamed back. There was a vacant parking lot about ten feet away. I opened the car door and started steering and pushing to the right. Mom got from behind and pushed. Fortunately, the couple stuck behind us got out and helped us push. I thanked them. I was no longer blocking traffic. We walked up the hill to Walmart and called my stepfather to come get us. My $100 car ended up needing an $800 transmission. Still, it was cheaper than a new car.

Lookout
(Memory #12)

As one would imagine, the southwest corner of
Wisconsin is not littered with gay men. There was
UW-Platteville, which was a half hour away and then
there was Madison in the opposite direction. These
were my choices to look for a boyfriend. I found a
personal ad for a guy my age studying at UWP,
exchanged photos and agreed to meet up at a local park,
just outside of Platteville. There was this secluded
lookout tower there that we could use. He said he
wasn't comfortable inviting me to his dorm room. I
understood. I didn't want him in my apartment either.

I pulled up to the only car in the parking lot. It was
quarter to 1 A.M. I got out and went over to the parked
car. He got out too.

"Are you Kyle?" he asked. He was beautiful. Jet-
black, curly hair, baby doll face, overweight but it
worked on him.

"Yes. Are you Andy?"

"Yup." We stood there for a few moments, in
silence. "You want to follow me?" I nodded and we
both got in our cars and headed into the woods. This
was going to be either very hot, or I was going to end
up as a lampshade back at his apartment, I thought.

Out of our cars, we stopped at the base of the lookout
tower, a tall, dark brown structure that pierced the sky
full of stars. The moon was full and provided the

perfect amount of light. The tower had been used to watch for forest fires back in the day.

"You first," he said.

"Why is that?"

"I want to look at that ass." I smiled and started climbing the stairs. I felt his hand cup one of my cheeks and then the other. I was completely out of breath by the time we reached the top. "C'mere," he said, pulling me in and we kissed. It felt good to be kissed and touched, like a century had passed since the last such encounter.

"You're a great kisser," he whispered as we undressed. Our bare bodies stood in the moonlight. A breeze blew by and I trembled a little.

"I'll warm you," he said. Lying on my clothes, he got on top of me. I ran my hands through his hair as we made out. I didn't really care if it went further. I was with someone I was attracted to, who seemed attracted to me and I was receiving affection. "Stand up," he said guiding me over to the corner, rolling hills spread out in all directions. He kissed the back of my neck as he entered me. I winced at first, but then it felt amazing. I gripped the railing until he was finished. He kissed the back of my neck again as we got dressed.

"Can I ask you something?" he said. Seriously? Now? It seemed like that should have happened earlier.

"Yes," I said with a hesitation.

"Can I see you again? I had fun and would like to do this again." I walked over and kissed him.

"Yes. I'd like that."

Andy became my regular hookup. Every couple of weeks, I'd receive an email from him and would drive down to Platteville. Eventually, he felt comfortable enough to have me over to his dorm. He never did come to my apartment, despite my repeated offers.

I liked Andy. I didn't know much about him, though. He was an Agriculture Sciences major, came from a long line of farmers and was expected to apply his studies back on the family farm. He voted for President Clinton and always had Diet Coke in his small cube shaped fridge. I had worked up the courage to ask Andy out after our next tryst. Sweaty, lying next to each other in his bed, he surprised me. "I can't see you again."

"What?" I said, thinking of my plans to court him.

"I can't keep doing this." He went on to tell me how he needed to find Jesus and his parents would never allow this behavior on the farm. I pulled up my jeans and put on my t-shirt. I smelled like him. I didn't know what to say, so I left. I didn't see Andy again for another year when I was flipping through the paper and saw his engagement photo. He was marrying the girl up the road from his farm. It read like a high school sweetheart story. I knew better.

Dick's Insider
(Memory #13)

When I wasn't spending my time sewing, it was spent watching old movies. Every Friday, I would cash my check, grab a few bottles of wine and pick out three VHS tapes. The local grocery store, Dick's, had a Chinese restaurant, liquor store and video store all connected to the main store. I could get everything I needed in one stop. I would go back the following day to return the three movies and pick out three more, get more wine and crispy garlic beef.

I worked my way through the section titled classics. I then took on the mystery and suspense category. My all-time favorite film is Hitchcock's *Rebecca*. When there was a film I couldn't find at Dick's, I would check it out from the library. I liked watching the old movies, not only because of the films, but they were readily available and in excellent condition. I often thought it was strange that there was such a comprehensive collection of great films, sitting there at a grocery store in Dodgeville.

Like most grocery stores, Dick's had a member rewards program called The Insider, an apparent nod to inside deals, coupons and savings. I got my card at the service desk and laughed. What marketing idiot came up with the name? I giggled like a thirteen-year-old boy every time the cashier asked if I had my Dick's Insider card.

I still have my card to this day. Never gets old. Here's photographic proof:

Trailer Park
(Memory #14)

Neal and I agreed to meet at Pizza Hut in Platteville for our first date. Not exactly Paris, but it had been forever since I had a date, so I couldn't be picky. I put on my favorite navy rollneck sweater, chinos and hopped in the Rabbit. I arrived five minutes early so I waited for him inside.

"Kyle?" he asked as he approached. He was wearing a sports jersey of some kind. I wasn't up on who played for what team. I couldn't even tell you what sport it was for. He had on ratty looking jeans and sneakers that I think were white at one time. Best foot forward?

"Yes! How are you, Neal?" I asked while shaking his hand. Despite the lack of style, he was cute. He had a boyish face that made you feel like you could trust him, blue eyes that were almost grey and short brown hair.

"I'm great now I'm here with you," he said sweetly. Ok. He was quickly making up lost points.

The hostess showed us to a booth in the corner. It was really dead for a Saturday night. We both ordered Diet Coke's and looked over the menu, despite both of us having it memorized. We ordered a large cheese pan pizza.

"So, how's college going?" I asked. He was studying Civil Engineering.

"It's going well. I can't complain." His Midwestern

accent was thick. I smiled. "What about you? What's it like to work at Roads' End?" Half of the county worked there. He knew the answer.

"It's ok. I've made a ton of friends there though. That's been the best part."

"Cool," he said, nodding. I would easily have dismissed him, thinking he was straight. I liked this about him.

We didn't speak much while we ate our pizza. I could feel his knee touching mine under the table. Neither of us moved.

After dinner, I insisted that I pay, that he was a college student and I was out there in the "real world." He finally relented. Outside, it started to rain. We couldn't decide what to do, so we got in his car. He had made a tape of the Spice Girls in honor of me and put it in the tape player. It made me laugh.

"What do you want to do?" I asked.

"I don't care. What do you want to do?" he served back to me.

Our heads turned at the same time and joined in a kiss. He placed his hand on my neck and gently stroked it with his thumb. We made out for a while, in the rain, in the Pizza Hut parking lot. Things started to get steamy, but we decided that we would take it slow. I got out of his car and got into mine. I waved to Neal, but I don't think he saw as his windows were fogged over. I pulled out of the parking lot and headed home.

The following week, we met at Pizza Hut again and pretty much the same date played out. After dinner, in the parking lot, we decided that we would go back to his place. He had, very sweetly, rented *Spice World* from Dick's grocery store in Platteville. I was dying to see it.

"Why don't you follow me in your car?" he suggested and I got in the Rabbit. He turned left out of the parking lot and headed towards Belmont, past Walmart and K-Mart and the new taco place that just went up. I wondered where he lived. It hadn't come up in our conversations. That was usually the first thing I asked; roommates or parents were always avoided. I turned off the radio as his car started slowing down and his left blinker was flashing.

There it was. The trailer park. I followed Neal around a circle shaped road to the very back where he parked his car in front of a brown trailer with tan trim. He got out of his car with a huge smile on his face. "Isn't it cool?" he said, holding up a hand like it was a prize on a game show.

"Very," I mustered as best I could. "Do you live here alone?"

"Yup! My parents figured buying this trailer was cheaper than dorms or an apartment." While I appreciated their economic position, I wasn't in love with the trailer. I had spent the better part of my youth in one, before my parent's divorce.

"C'mon!" he welcomed me in.

His place was very nice. I was expecting a crack den,

but found new furniture, purchased from Walmart or K-Mart down the road, I thought. It smelled new. I liked that. It was a still a trailer, but at least it didn't smell like one.

Neal offered me to help myself to a Diet Coke in the fridge while he put the tape in the VCR. I joined him on the sofa. He put his hand on my knee were he kept it for the entire film.

Spice World was great. Everything I wanted it to be. After it was done, he clicked the T.V. off and turned to me, hand inching higher on my thigh and landing on my erection. We started kissing and then he led me down a narrow hallway to the very rear of the trailer, his bedroom.

We undressed each other as we stood kissing at the foot of his bed. Fully naked, we fell back, him landing on top of me. After we were finished, we laid in bed in silence. I could see the taillights of the traffic as it whizzed by on the highway. Neal gently stroked my arm.

"That was great," he said, not looking at me.

"Yeah, that was," I concurred. Not sure of what to do next, I said I was going to head out.

"You sure? You're welcome to stay the night." I knew how trailer parks worked. I could see people peeking through their curtains and blinds, shaking their heads at me as I got in my car and drove away.

"Yeah, I have brunch tomorrow with my family." A lie.

"Ok." He stayed in bed as I got up and got dressed. I sat back down on the bed and kissed him goodbye.

As I drove out of the trailer park, I shuddered. I never fully knew the circumstances surrounding why we sold our big house on Maiden Street and moved into a trailer outside of Mineral Point. I only remember a vague shame about it.

I always felt like a second-class citizen living there. I would overhear kids at school as they made fun of the trailer park residents. I also felt guilty for feeling like I was better than a trailer park, such class warfare for a thirteen-year-old.

Maybe it was the trailer. Or the sports jerseys. Or the nasty sneakers. Or the memories that the trailer park conjured. Maybe it was a combination of it all, but I never saw Neal again.

Casino Royale

Grandma was a night owl. She never used to be until Grandpa passed away. Then, she ended up staying up all night chatting with people and playing games on the computer. She even took to learning how to touch up and edit digital photos. I was impressed.

I tossed and turned on the sofa in the front room of her house. Nothing there had changed in thirty years. I couldn't sleep. I kept thinking about returning to my apartment back in New York, to find a pile of bills, rent due and no job prospects. I could see the kitchen light on and smell the smoke from her cigarette.

"Can't sleep?" she asked as I entered the kitchen and flopped down at the table. I noticed the clock read 2:46 A.M.

"No," I said, looking at all of the sugar-free products she had across the room. She developed diabetes late in life and had a sweet tooth. Not a great combination. "You?" I asked.

"Nope," she said, continuing to click on whatever she was working on. I couldn't see from where I was sitting. "You want to go down to the track?"

By track she meant the dog track. And by dog track, she meant the casino at the dog track. "Sure," I said. "Just let me change."

Around 3 A.M., we climbed in her truck and headed towards Dubuque. An hour later we pulled into the parking lot. I think we took another twenty minutes to find the closest spot near the entrance. Her legs weren't what they used to be, she told me.

"Here," she said, handing me a crisp new hundred-dollar bill. "For gambling. I'll meet you back out here in an hour. Deal?"

"Deal," I said, holding the door open for her. Inside was another world entirely. It was a sea of old people and what looked like ex-cons. Everyone was smoking and staring intently at the slot machines in front of them. There was an occasional cheer from someone who hit a jackpot. It was all so foreign to me. I looked around and Grandma was gone. I hadn't seen which direction she had gone. I suspected she had a favorite machine and was going to start there.

"Drink?" said a pretty, perky blond girl. A drink. That's exactly what I needed.

"Yes! How much do I owe you?" I asked, taking the plastic cup from her tray.

"Silly boy!" she said. "Drinks are free!" and walked away. What? What was this? Had I just discovered the Holy Grail? Free drinks? I made my way to the back of the room where the bar was. For the next hour, I slammed screwdrivers made with cheap vodka and no-name orange juice.

At the appointed time, I met Grandma back out in front of the casino. "So," she said, lighting another cigarette. "How'd you do?"

"I have one hundred dollars."

"Lucky! You broke even. I lost two hundred!"

"Oh, I didn't gamble."

"Huh?" she said, stopping in her tracks.

"See, the way I look at it was I was walking out tonight with more than I came in with. I wasn't going to chance that." She busted out laughing.

"Oh, Kyle. I love you."

"Love you too, Grandma." I offered to give her the bill back. She insisted I keep it. We stopped at the gas station back in Mineral Point and she bought us fresh muffins and coffee.

Friday Night Special
(Memory #15)

Every night after work, I would return to my apartment
and sit in front of the T.V. Friday night was
different. It felt like committing a crime to be at
home. Especially when spring rolled around. After I
had exhausted the video rental at Dick's, each Friday
after work, I would get in the Rabbit and head to
Madison in an effort to find a boyfriend. I would make
sure to dress up that day. I needed all the help I could
get. As I am naturally a homebody, this was the perfect
way to get myself out there.

Bypassing my usual exit, I continued on Highway 151
until it brought me into Fitchburg and then into
Madison. Pulling up in front of Canterbury Tales, a
bookstore and café, I found a spot to park. Parking in
downtown Madison can be frustrating, but I always
managed to find a spot on Friday night.

Canterbury Tales was just off State Street, the main
drag for college kids. I figured if I were to meet
someone, this would be the place. Each week, the same
scenario would play out, I would get my usual table
near the window, I'd order a coffee and a vegetarian
chili (I'm not a vegetarian, I just love chili and it was
the only one they had on the menu) and I would chat
with my waiter, Paul. Paul was studying Art History at
the UW. He was tall, overweight, curly brown hair,
nerdy glasses and a killer smile. He was perfect. We
would flirt with each other as I sipped my coffee and
ate my chili.

This went on for about two months when I finally decided to ask him out. He said yes. I couldn't believe it. Yes! He said yes! The plan was to meet the following week. He would take off work and we would go out to dinner and drinks. While I usually sing in the car, that night, I didn't even turn the radio on. I allowed myself to be happy, soak in the prospect of finding love. I decided not to take my usual way home. I wasn't in a hurry anyway. Just the stars, the winding back roads, and me.

Next week couldn't come fast enough. When it did, I zipped up to Madison as quickly as I could. Noodles & Company was our designated meeting spot. Not the fanciest of first dates, but it was one of my favorite places to eat. I didn't see Paul so I stood near the front door, studying the menu, which I knew by heart. Twenty minutes passed and still no date. I waited another ten minutes and decided to walk over to Canterbury Tales.

"Hi," I said to the hostess, Kim, whom I had seen so many Friday nights. She seemed nervous, definitely not herself. "Say, is Paul here?"

"Umm, Paul moved to California," she blurted out.

"What?" I said in complete disbelief.

"Yeah, he has family there and he had to move back." She turned and bolted for the kitchen. I turned and sulked out the door. Seriously? I thought. Was that really the best excuse? And if he really was moving to California on such short notice, why didn't he call or email me? Why stand me up at one of my favorite restaurant chains? Now I will never be able to eat there again.

That was the last time I set foot in Canterbury Tales. I thought about calling and asking for him or popping in unannounced to catch him in the lie. Focusing on the bottle of Stoli I had at home in my freezer, I decided to let it go.

Lounge Lizard Oasis
(Memory #16)

There was a resurgence of the 1960s happening and I jumped on board full force. From the music to the interiors and even the clothing, kitsch was in. And I owned it. In my apartment, I made leopard print throw pillows for the futon and my favorite chair, I made a faux zebra hide rug for the living room, and I bought every CD in the *Ultra-Lounge* series. I learned to make martinis that Dean Martin would have been proud of. I even found a very trim navy suit at a thrift store in Madison. It had very narrow lapels and I wore it whenever I could. I even wore it to see Tom Jones live in Wisconsin Dells.

My apartment was very masculine in feel. I framed some of my favorite black and white photos in black frames and hung them against the cream walls. The bedding covering the futon was cream and black gingham checks and ticking stripes. I upholstered my favorite chair with cream-colored muslin. I couldn't find an ottoman that I liked, so I just pulled over the bench from the piano when I wanted to put my feet up. Black towels hung in the bathroom (big mistake as they fade and collect lint) next to a vinyl tortoise patterned shower curtain. I usually kept fresh cut flowers on my kitchen table.

While I worked in the apartment, Bobby Darin would play on the stereo. I had fallen head over heels in love with his voice. I bought every CD I could find. I loved his version of *A Nightingale Sang in Berkley Square*. Sometimes it was on repeat. As I washed dishes, I would swing my hips and sing along. I had amassed quite the martini glass collection. Almost anyone who knew me always gave me different ones, in all shapes, sizes and colors as gifts. I even received a set of mini ones as Christmas ornaments.

On the sole glass-topped end table next to the futon, I had a black halogen arm lamp that cast a soft glow over the entire apartment. I almost always had candles burning in frosted votive holders in each of the windowsills and on the tank of the toilet. Some nights, I would sit in my favorite chair, wine in hand, and watch the moving shadows they created.

I had always been sensitive to my living space. I felt like the rest of my family could be cave dwellers and be perfectly happy. Not me. I preferred to create tranquil, clean, spaces that reflected my interests and me. Be it a dorm room or an apartment, I always formed a little oasis for myself. Sometimes, I go back to that apartment, in my mind, and walk around. Touching the surfaces and breathing in its scent, somewhere between Earl Grey Tea and fresh paint, I remember how at home I felt there.

In a Galaxy Far, Far Away...
(Memory #17)

I watched the clock in the lower right hand of my computer click 3:30 P.M. Quitting time. I went over to Adam's desk where I found him putting a Coltrane CD back into its jewel case.

"You ready?" I asked.

"You know it," he said. We put our time slips on our manager's desk and walked out to the parking lot. Friday night. Our plan was to take his car and leave mine there. He just bought a brand new Mercury Cougar in bright red metallic paint. Way nicer than the Rabbit. We were headed to Madison to see the new *Star Wars* movie, have dinner and then drinks downtown.

I clicked my seatbelt into place. "What do you want to listen to?" he asked. I took Garbage's Version 2.0 out of my bag and handed it to him. "Nice," he responded. Adam was one of my best and most unlikely of friends. We met during training and I was terrified of him. He was short, obviously straight and I didn't think he liked me much. I avoided him for a good six months. Then one day, I saw a Miles Davis CD sitting on his desk. I asked to borrow it and we were friends ever since.

We pulled into Marcus Cinemas on the west side of Madison with plenty of time to get our tickets and choose the best seats. We were both huge *Star Wars* fans and it was opening day and we were not leaving it to chance. We chose seats in the middle of the theater up towards the back. Some high school kids heckled us about being on a date. "Shut the fuck up or I'll punch your fucking face in," Adam said standing up, defending my honor. He was incredibly protective of me. I liked being out with him for that reason. I also loved teasing him when people thought we were a couple.

Midway through the film, Adam leaned in. "You want to go? I can't take this."

"Yeah, it's pretty bad, but we're here, let's finish it," I said. He sighed. It was true. I was there, awful or not, I was finishing it. After the movie, he just shook his head as we walked to the car.

"That was a huge piece of shit," he said.

"I agree. Let's eat." We headed to TGI Friday's. The hostess sat us in what looked to be a sunroom off the main dining/bar area. I was starving and knew that I was going to make sweet love to a giant plate of chicken fingers with ranch dressing. Our waitress came over and introduced herself.

"Hey guys, I'm Peggy. I'll be taking care of you tonight. Can I get you started with something to drink?"

"Jameson on the rocks," Adam said.

"Stoli martini, straight up with a twist," I said.

"You're fancy!" she said, patting me on the

shoulder. Peggy, shirt covered in buttons, tattooed arms and many visible piercings, I was sure, was not fancy.

"I think Peggy likes you," Adam said, kicking me under the table. I laughed it off.

"Here you go." She returned with the drinks and took our dinner order, again patting me on the shoulder. Adam and I toasted one another and sipped our drinks.

"What was up with Jar Jar Binks?" I asked.

"I was seriously hoping he'd get a light saber directly down the center of his head."

"Yeah. That was a kids' movie, clearly."

"Oh, man, you're never gonna believe this," he said with excitement, like he just unwrapped a new toy.

"This is going to be good," I said.

"So, my buddy Tom got really drunk last weekend. I'm talking alcohol poisoning drunk. And decided he was going to make a porno film." I busted out laughing. "No, wait, it gets better. So, he calls up this hooker and asks her if she wants to be in the film, saying he'll pay her. And she agrees!" I loved where this story was headed.

"So, she comes over to his place and he has the camera all set up on the tripod. He pays her and they start going. He's taking her from behind while she's on all fours."

"Ok…" I said, waiting for the punch line.

"And so, he's going at it like hardcore right? Then he fucking pukes all over her back! She jumps up screaming; puke running off her back, falling everywhere. Oh, man you have to see it."

I busted out laughing. "You mean you have the tape?"

"Yup," he said proudly.

"I think I'm good." I said, still laughing.

Shortly, Peggy returned with our food. And Peggy was chatty. "So, what are you boys doing tonight?"

"We just saw the new *Star Wars* movie and are going out after this," Adam offered.

"Cool. I'm working 'til midnight. Got a sitter for tomorrow night, though. Going to Weedstock." We both just nodded at her. "Enjoy," she said with a wink directed at me.

"Dude, she wants you," Adam teased.

"Yeah, she's just my type."

When the check came, she handed it to me with another wink. On the back, in the curliest cursive I had ever seen was: "*Call me! 608-937-8663*." I turned it over to show Adam.

"What the fuck? What if you and I were on a date?"

"Seriously? You're jealous of Peggy and her child? Are you afraid I'm going to leave you for her and go to Weedstock?" I left a good tip and pocketed the receipt. I never got hit on. Ever. Even if this was a trashy woman and not a hot guy, I was saving this trophy.

We ended up downtown at The Great Dane Brewery. We had a fair amount of alcohol at TGI Friday's and were ready to continue. We found two stools at the bar and Adam ordered Jameson and I stuck with martinis.

"I think that woman is looking at you," he whispered to me as inconspicuously as possible.

"Nah," I said. I looked across the bar. She looked like Lara Flynn Boyle. Jet-black hair tucked behind her ears, fitted black dress, string of white pearls. She looked out of place in Wisconsin and definitely more my type than Peggy. We made eye contact a few times and Adam kept hitting my thigh with his hand.

Three martinis later, she stood up, fixed her dress and walked over to me. "Hello," she said, leaning one arm on my shoulder.

"Hi, I'm Kyle."

"Katie," she said sweetly. "What are you drinking?"

"Stoli martini."

"I love a man who drinks martinis."

I almost said "me too." Instead, I offered her one,

which she accepted with a nod. She asked the
bartender for a pen. She took a napkin from the back of
the bar and scribbled her number on it and handed it to
me.

"Thanks for the drink, Kyle." And she walked back to
her seat.

"Seriously, what is going on tonight?" Adam asked.

"I'm on fire," I said. Katie took the last sip of her
martini and waved us goodbye.

"Yeah you are." One more martini later, we stumbled
out to Adam's car. After that, I don't remember
anything until I heard Adam say: "Oh, shit." I was
slumped down in the seat, but could see the red and
blue flashing lights. "Oh, shit."

The officer tapped on the window. Adam reluctantly
rolled it down. "License and registration,
please." Adam again reluctantly, handed them to
him. "Say, you boys been drinking?"

"No, sir," Adam said.

"What's wrong with your friend?"

"He's tired. Actually, he's too drunk to drive, so I am
taking him home."

"That's nice of you. Take it slower, huh?" He handed
Adam back his license and let us go. It turns out Adam
got lucky that night, too.

What's That Smell?
(Memory #18)

My friend Anka had just moved into a new studio apartment in Madison and I was on my way to see it, a housewarming party for two. I made my way down John Nolan Drive and turned a few exits before downtown. Two stoplights later, I found the address.

"Sparky!" I said as I exited my car. She was outside waiting for me. I always called her Sparky. She called me Evol, which is love spelled backwards. I never really remember why or how that got started.

"Evol! You found it!" I ran up and hugged her.

"Let's get inside. You must be freezing!" I moved my hand up and down her back in a gesture to warm her. She was beautiful. One of the most beautiful people I had known, inside and out. Her parents were from Denmark, but she was raised in the U.S. She easily stood at six feet tall, had a model's body and face and was wildly creative.

"I didn't want you to miss the house!" It was kind of set back and there were trees out front, but I had no problems.

"Oh, my God! I love it!" I said upon entering the apartment. Her studio felt very European. Something out of an Anthropologie catalog. Bohemian, lived in, and very contemporary. Many of her painted canvasses lined the walls and on the floor beneath, leaning on the wall. She had a canvas on the easel, but she wouldn't let me see it. "So, what are we doing for your big housewarming?" I asked, sitting down on the most beautiful antique wooden chair.

"Well, I thought we'd get pizza from The Glass Nickel and drink."

"That's my girl," I said and she cracked up. "What do you have to drink?" I helped myself to her fridge. It was stocked full of Carlsberg Elephant Beer. "What's this?" I held up a bottle.

"It's beer from Denmark."

"Oh, cool," I said; helping myself to the bottle opener in the first drawer I opened. Oh, we'd be the perfect couple, I thought. I knew exactly where everything was because we often shared a brain. Alas, that wasn't in the cards. I took a sip and made a face.

"Yeah, it takes some getting used to," Anka said, getting a beer for herself. She then put the *Thunderball* VHS tape into the player. She and I were huge James Bond fans. We knew all the lines to every movie and countless pieces of random trivia.

"Excellent choice," I said, chugging the last of my beer.

"Whoa, killer!" she said as I got up and got another beer. It had been a long week at Roads' End. I was ready to put it behind me.

I had easily put away a six-pack when we decided to order pizza. We both favored plain, cheese pizza. Another reason we were perfectly matched. I had never had pizza from The Glass Nickel, but she swore by it so I trusted her. Twenty minutes later, dinner arrived.

"This is really good!" I said, grabbing a second slice.

"Told you." Anka got up and put *Goldfinger* into the VCR.

"Another great choice," I said. Anka was catching up to me with the number of beers she had. We were both inching towards fourteen bottles each. After the movie ended, she insisted that I stay the night and not drive intoxicated back to Mineral Point. I brought an overnight bag to that end.

I changed into my sweatpants and Gap t-shirt and crawled into her bed. It was pressed against the wall. I could feel heat radiating from the electric floorboard heater. I took the side next to the wall. Anka came out from the bathroom having put her pajamas on and climbed into bed. She instantly passed out. I on the other hand, did not feel well. The room began to spin. I tried to talk myself out of being sick, but it was of no use. I threw my head to the side and barfed, all down her wall and into the heater. I plopped back down, too drunk to get out of bed and rinse my mouth out.

A few minutes went by and I thought I was going to be ok. Then I threw my head to the right again, as if I had no control over my body and vomited a second time. This round did the trick and I passed out almost immediately as Anka had.

The next day, we didn't get out of bed until around 3 P.M., when Anka made her way to the fridge and got us Gatorade. It wasn't until around 7 P.M. that I was able to get up, brush my teeth and get back in my car and head home. It was truly up there in the hangover hall of fame.

A month and a half later, I got an email from Anka inviting me over to her new apartment. She had broken the lease on the studio apartment as every time she'd turn on the heat, all she could smell was vomit. I wasn't allowed to drink at the new place.

Hijinks, In Memoriam

"Hi Grandma," I said as I closed the kitchen door. I set the Walgreen's bag on her kitchen table. I needed deodorant, toothpaste and Listerine for my visit. Grandma had dentures and no need to keep toothpaste in the house.

"Hey," she said, not looking up from the newspaper. I took off my coat and sat down next to her. *The Addams Family* was on T.V. I watched as she continued to read. The house seemed to be in more disrepair than last time. Holes in screens, wallpaper peeling, a piece of trim missing on the kitchen doorframe. Ever since my grandfather passed away, she had no interest in maintaining their house. It always made me sad. It didn't seem to bother her much.

"Did you eat?" she asked, folding the newspaper and setting in on a stack of previously read ones.

"Nope," I said.

"You want to grab a bite at the Pointer Café?"

"Sure," I said. We put on our coats and headed out to her truck. The Pointer Café was a tiny restaurant on the old highway. It was where the locals went for cheap fare. Grandma liked it mainly because her friends all ate there so she could catch up on the town gossip. It wouldn't have been my first choice, but I knew it made her happy and she was quite picky about her food. Anything too fancy or containing too many spices and she was done.

"Thank you," I said as I took the menu from the waitress and turned my coffee mug right side up, indicating I wanted it filled.

"Do you want to hear about our specials?" she asked.

"Sure," Grandma said.

"Well, tonight we have breaded cod and fries for $8.99 and chicken and biscuits for $9.99."

"That's what I'll have!" she said with excitement. Grandma's favorite meal was chicken and biscuits.

"And for you?" This left me no time to look over the menu.

"Um, I'll have chicken fingers and fries." I blurted out, assuming it was on the menu. The waitress scribbled on her pad and walked away. I guess I was in luck.

"Are you going to see anyone while you're home?" Grandma asked.

"I am going to call Adam after Thanksgiving. That's about it. If I run into someone, then maybe. I am really just home to see you and the family." She smiled. The waitress returned with a Diet Pepsi for Grandma.

Our food arrived and we quietly ate. She was in comfort food heaven. Occasionally, friends of hers would stop and say hi and asked about my whereabouts and employment status. I lied to all of them. Dinner couldn't end fast enough. I kept telling myself that Grandma needed this. That it wasn't about me.

After dinner we pulled into the IGA parking
lot. Grandma wanted to get a few groceries for the
house. I wandered up and down the aisles by myself,
remembering when I worked there. I stopped by the
canned peas and busted out laughing. One time, in the
backroom, where we put dented and damaged products,
there was a can of Alpo dog food that was missing its
label. Very carefully, I removed the label from a can of
peas and affixed it to the dog food and set it back out
for sale. A few weeks later, we had a very angry
customer returning the opened can. I couldn't stop
laughing.

There was the PA system that the cashiers used to call
one of the stock guys to come carry groceries out to
someone's car. One of us always managed to get on it
and say something inappropriate while the last straggler
of a customer was in the store.

"What are you smiling at?" Grandma asked with a grin.

"Oh, nothing. Just remembering when I worked here."

"Hasn't changed much, has it?" I shook my head no. I
looked at the cashier and the stock guy bagging up the
groceries. Did I look that young when I was here? I
asked myself.

Back in the truck, Grandma asked if I wouldn't mind
going over to the cemetery to put some fake flowers on
Grandpa's grave. I said sure. I hoped that when I died,
no one would put tacky fake flowers on my grave.

She pulled into Graceland Cemetery off Fair
Street. The road sloped downhill and to the left. That's

where his grave was and an empty plot next to him for her. I was torn between thinking that was sweet and touching and morbid and creepy. I took the bright blue fake flowers from behind the seat and helped Grandma walk over to the grave. I divided the flowers and put them uniformly in each of the metal urns on either side of the grave marker.

After Grandpa passed away, my aunts and uncles stopped coming around. It broke Grandma's heart. She was my grandmother by marriage. She married my grandfather just after I was born. To me, she always was and will be Grandma. The rest of my family, save my father and brother, didn't feel the same.

"I sure miss him," Grandma said starting to sob and I put my arm around her. "I…sure…miss him," she repeated.

"I know, Grandma. I know."

Picture Perfect
(Memory #19)

I could see the camera equipment surrounding the desk at the end of the aisle, near the mini kitchen. Adam was headed in my direction.

"Dude, you got the shaft."

"Good morning to you, too. What's with all of the camera equipment?" He didn't answer me. I approached the cube, taking off my coat as I did. There was Greg, the most beautiful guy in our department. He looked like the picture perfect guy next-door type. He was sitting with a toothy smile, holding up a polo shirt. On the screen behind him, was an elaborate logo for home improvement chain that I had digitized. On the polo shirt was the final result. It was all starting to come into focus.

My boss, Cheryl, immediately intercepted me. "Kyle, look, come with me and I'll explain." The crew continued to snap shots of Greg. Greg the imposter.

Cheryl closed the door to the conference room. Neither of us sat. "This was not my decision to photograph Greg for the catalog with your work. It really wasn't. The art directors felt that he has mass appeal." Tears were starting to collect in my eyelids. I was determined not to cry in front of her.

"No problem," I said, leaving the room without continuing the discussion. I went to my cube and turned on my computer. I wanted a cup of coffee, but didn't want to return to the scene of the crime. I emailed Adam and asked if he would bring me one. He did.

"You ok?" asked June.

"I'll be fine. I should have expected as much." She rubbed my back for a minute and returned to her cube. My inner circle of CAD friends, one by one, made their way over to make sure I was ok. Last but not least, Greg.

"Look man, I'm really sorry about this. It wasn't my idea. They asked and I said..." I held up my hand cutting him off. I didn't say a word. I opened a file to digitize. He stood there for a few seconds and finally left. My motivation to do work worthy of a catalog spread was gone.

Promptly at 3:30 P.M., I shut down my computer and left. Back at my apartment, I poured an ice-cold martini and sat down at my computer. I slowly sipped it as I waited for the modem to make a connection. I was in desperate need of validation. What better place to find it than on the Internet!

I joined a very snarky chat room full of very funny and bitchy guys. I read their comments and laughed as I drank my martini. They playful teased and jabbed one another as I sat, voyeur style, and watched it play out.

A window popped up on my screen. It was a private chat. From a guy named Jerry.

> *Jerry: Hi! How's it going?*
> *Kyle: Great. You?*

Jerry: Good! What are you up to?
Kyle: Martini number three.
Jerry: Haha. I am having a scotch.
Kyle: Very nice.
Jerry: What do you do?
Kyle: I'm a CAD designer. You?
Jerry: I'm a computer programmer.
Kyle: Very cool. Where do you live?
Jerry: Madison, well, Fitchburg to be exact. You?
Kyle: Mineral Point, southwest of Madison.
Jerry: I've been through there. You want to exchange pics?
Kyle: Ok. You first.

I saw the progress bar move from left to right. I sat with anticipation. His picture was soon in the chat window. He was hot. Or at least the person in this photo was hot. He had sandy blond hair, a huge angled nose, full lips, dimples and eyes somewhere between blue and green. The photo could easily have served as a headshot for a wannabe actor.

Kyle: Very nice.
Jerry: Now you.

Nervously, I dragged a jpeg of me to the chat window and released it. Again, I watched as the progress bar hit 100%. I took a sip of my martini and said a little prayer that he would like me. I waited a bit for a response but didn't get one. Maybe he had to go to the bathroom or was refilling his glass with scotch. Nothing but the blinking cursor moved on the screen.

Kyle: So?

Almost as quickly as I typed it, he exited out of the chat session. I covered my face and began to sob. Mid-cry, I knocked my martini glass over. As the top broke away from the stem, the martini sprayed all over my t-shirt. I threw the pieces in the trash, changed my shirt and cried myself to sleep.

At work, I couldn't stop thinking about the betrayal by my boss and Greg. I couldn't let it go. It was one thing to be rejected anonymously over the Internet, but an entirely other thing to be told you're too ugly to be featured in a catalog shoot.

For the next couple of weeks, I pretty much kept to myself and let it stew. I was good at that. Adam, June, Mona and Jan all tried their best to bring me out of my funk. Nothing worked. One day, while filling up my Roads' End logoed coffee mug, I saw a posting for an internal candidate for a fit model. The corporate sales division was upgrading the fit and quality of the clothing and they needed a guy and a girl to try on the samples and wear them and provide feedback.

Back at my desk, I went on the Intranet and applied. This brightened my spirits a little. Something on the horizon. Something to look forward to. Something to tell me I was good enough. The following week, I saw an email come through from Human Resources. I didn't get the fit model job.

"You got shafted twice by Greg," Adam said as he stood outside my cube, coffee mug in hand.

"Huh?" I said, turning from my computer.

"Greg got the fit model job."

"You've got to be fucking kidding me."

"Nope," he said, sipping his coffee.

I fired off an email back to H.R. asking, demanding really, why I was not selected. I received the following response:

> *Kyle,*
>
> *We are so sorry we were not able to offer you the position of fit model for Corporate Sales. We have very strict measurement requirements to ensure our clothing offerings are of the highest quality. Please keep checking back on the Intranet for other opportunities.*
>
> *Best,*
> *Human Resources*

Everyone in the department knew that I applied for and wanted that position. I filled out my time card and told my boss I wasn't feeling well and was taking a half of a sick day. I went to Culver's and stuffed myself with chicken fingers with ranch dressing, deep fried cheese curds and the biggest Diet Pepsi they had.

Two months later, there was a posting for a CAD designer with the tailored clothing department. I would be designing plaids, prints, stripes and other patterns for the tailored clothing designers. The position was for six months while the current CAD designer went on maternity leave. Just about everyone in our department wanted the gig. I knew this would be an amazing opportunity for me to add additional pieces to my portfolio as well as have another level of experience in the apparel world. I applied immediately.

"If I don't get this, I'm going to light the office on fire," I said to Mona and June as we sat in the break room. It was pizza day. On Wednesdays, Pizza Hut came and set up an all-you-can-eat pizza buffet.

"You will. I have a good feeling about this," said Mona.

"Third time's a charm!" added June.

They were right. After two interviews, I got the position. Like the song goes: you can't always get what you want. But, you might just get what you need.

The Other Woman
(Memory #20)

Deciding to give online dating another shot, I logged onto my computer. I sipped an ice-cold martini and stared at the perfectly curled lemon peel floating amongst the crystals. The modem screeched and pinged. Damn, I'm good, I thought. Having navigated to a dating site, I decided to search for Mineral Point. Usually a futile endeavor, but I would start there and work my way out. To my surprise, I found one listing.

> *Married and lonely.*
> *I'm 34, married, good build and clean.*
> *Need to be discreet.*

I decided to respond. I didn't love the idea of being the other woman, but I was single and lonely and living in a town with zero prospects. Two martinis later, he responded.

> *Hi Kyle,*
>
> *Thanks for writing. As I said, I'm married and this must be discreet. I hope that works for you. Can you send your photo and I will send mine back?*
>
> *Best,*
> *Rob*

I replied with my photo and an agreement his secret was safe with me. He wrote back with his photo. He was very dashing. I pictured women hitting on him all the time. He looked very masculine, reddish blond hair brushed back, stubble beard with the occasional grey hair, trim body and dark eyes that definitely had a story behind them.

We agreed to meet. Obviously, he would come to my place. He was actually only a few blocks away from me, so he walked. Soon, there was a knock on the door. It all happened so quickly.

"Hi," I said, opening the door and realizing that I had had too many martinis.

"Hi, Kyle," he said, entering my apartment.

"Sorry, it's not much." I don't know why I said that.

"No, this is great." He held out a bottle of wine. The label looked fancy. I took it from him and went to the counter and uncorked it. He sat down at my kitchen table and I brought the wine over with two glasses. It was clear he was very nervous. I don't know why I wasn't. I usually am at first meetings. I chocked it up to the martinis.

"So, what is it that you do?" I asked, pouring us each a glass.

"Well, I used to be an industrial designer."

"Why the past tense?" The wine was good.

"We moved here for my wife's job. I'm now the housewife."

"How that working out?" He made a face that suggested it wasn't his calling. "How long have you been in our little hamlet?"

"Six months."

"I'm surprised we haven't run into one another."

"Which leads me to say, please, if we see each other in public, please don't acknowledge that we know each other."

"I told you, I have no plan on sharing this info."

"Good," he said and took a sip of his wine. His foot found mine under the table. I got up and put Coltrane's *Blue Train* into the disc player. "A jazz lover, I see," he said as I sat back down at the table, his foot immediately finding mine again. We sat for a while, listening to the music and sipping our wine without speaking. As I poured us a second glass, he leaned in and kissed me. "Let's go to the sofa," he suggested.

I pushed aside the leopard print pillows to make room for us. He set his wine on the floor and took my head in his hands and passionately kissed me. One of his hands found my knee where it stayed for a few minutes before traveling up and under my boxer shorts. I was instantly hard at his touch. I set my wine on the floor and used my newly free hand to unbutton his dress shirt. I ran my hand across his ginger colored chest hair. He had the most beautiful pecs.

He pulled my shirt off and suddenly I was completely self-conscious of my body. He was in way better shape than I. He gently pushed me on my back and kissed my stomach. Then he lowered himself above my crotch and kissed my erection and slowly slid my boxers off. "Wow," he said, taking me in his mouth. For a straight guy, he was good at giving head.

I pulled him up on top of me and kissed him. As we made out, I unbuttoned his jeans and he slid them off. I did the same with his briefs. Then I felt it on my leg. His penis was easily half the size of mine. Now, don't get me wrong. I'm no size queen, but given his J.Crew catalog perfect image, I was expecting more.

After we finished, he asked if he could use the shower. I said of course and got him a clean towel to use. "When can I see you again?" he asked, pulling on his jeans.

"Any time you can sneak away." I hated saying that. But, he was lonely. I was lonely. We were only separated by a few blocks and a wife. I couldn't turn away this situation. He approached me and kissed me again. Not the simple, casual hookup kiss. This kiss felt like it came from somewhere special. I almost told him I loved him. I had no idea where that came from and was relieved I didn't say those words.

For the rest of the time I lived there, I saw Rob at least once a week. Same routine: wine, sex, and a shower. I was ok with this.

10%
(Memory #21)

"So, you'll go with me?" I wasn't yet at the begging stage. Close.

"I don't know."

"Sparky, c'mon! I don't want to go alone!"

"I'm just teasing! You get worked up so easily. You know I'll go." Anka loved pressing my buttons and I hers.

"Whew. Oh, I made the cutest party dress for you. Kelly green satin, spaghetti straps, hits at your knee."

"Evol! That sounds perfect." Every now and again, I would make clothes for Anka. She was pretty much a model, just needed the confidence and a contract. We now had plans to go to the spring 10% Society Dance. It was a chance for gay and lesbian teens and college-aged kids to meet. I thought I would give it a go despite my lackluster experiences with the bar scene and online dating. My hopes were low as I'm pretty much always the resident wallflower.

The 10% came from the notion that at least 10% of the population was gay or lesbian. I joked with Anka that there was a 10% chance I would meet someone. I felt bad for her, being straight and single at a gay dance. But, she loved music and dancing, so there was that.

Saturday night, I parked the Rabbit in front of Anka's apartment, garment bag in hand. I knocked on her door.

"Evol!" she exclaimed, nearly ripping the garment bag from my hand. She ran into her bathroom to slip into her new dress. It fit her like the proverbial glove. She came out of the bathroom with a mesmerized look on her face. "This is easily your best work. This dress is amazing." She slipped on a pair of stilettos, which made her tower over me. "Let's go," she said, taking my arm, *Un-break My Heart* played on the stereo.

The dance was held at the Memorial Union. The space was decorated with the requisite rainbow and pink streamers and balloons. Techno music blared from the auditorium. There was a marble lobby type space outside where several people congregated.

Anka was turning heads. All the lesbians wanted to be with her. All the gays wanted to know where she got her dress. I became the talk of several conversations as Anka pointed to me when she was asked about my green masterpiece.

"You made that?" asked white-bearded guy, easily three times my age.

"Yes, I did." I said politely. "I'm going to be a fashion designer."

"That's great. Buy you a drink?" His chances were less than 10%, but a drink sounded good. I insisted I would only take one if he bought Anka one, too. He returned moments later with some fruity drink, without any trace of alcohol.

"You know I'm old enough to drink," I said to my scruffy new friend. He laughed.

"You're a funny one! Of course there's booze in there." He moved in closer.

"Well, thank you for the drink. Anka and I need to find our friends. Thank you!" I said, almost pulling Anka with me as fast as I could.

"You're off to a great start." She elbowed me.

"Tell me about it." She was right. Another couple in their sixties came up to me and propositioned me for a three-way with them, in front of Anka. I declined, adding that it was insulting not to include her. Anka busted out laughing as we walked away from them. "What's with me? Let's get more drinks."

"That's going to be you one day," she joked. I punched her arm.

"Don't you dare say that," I said. We made our way to the bar and I bought us each two of the same fruity cocktails. We slammed them both down and I returned and made the same purchase. After that round was slammed, we were ready for some dancing.

Anka was actually a great dancer. I just sort of moved like I was having a seizure, completely self-conscious of my every movement. Lesbian after lesbian kept coming up to Anka on the dance floor. I would have too. She was easily the most beautiful woman there. I was jealous of her for a moment. She had less confidence than I did, but she had the looks. I did not.

I smiled at a guy I thought was cute as he was making his way towards us. He stopped, made a face like I had just puked on him and went the other way. I left Anka to her dancing and went to get more of that fruity elixir.

I sat down on a bench in that big marble room. I watched as couple after couple would leave the auditorium, hand in hand, in search of fun outside of dancing. I was suddenly panged with the feeling I got in gym class when I was the last to be picked for a team, each side begging for me to not join them.

I could see Anka dancing with a group of lesbians. She was having a blast. That made me smile. I wanted to be having a blast. What was wrong with me? I eked out another sip from the cup I was holding. I wanted something stronger. I wanted to go to Café Montmartre and drown myself in martinis.

A bald guy with a thick white mustache came up to me. "I'm waiting for my boyfriend." I lied. He turned and went to the next young guy in the room and offered up the same line, which was met with the same reaction. What was with all the old guys here? I thought.

Anka returned with three girls in her wake. "Hey! Do you want to go to a party? They're awesome!" she said, pointing to them.

"No," I said. "You go on without me. Call me tomorrow."

"Ok!" she said as they pulled her off in the opposite

direction. I made my way to the coat check and retrieved mine. I walked slowly up State Street towards the Capital and over to Café Montmartre, this dark, plain little bar off the square. Deep burgundy walls, art from local artists and thick velvet curtains just off the entry room defined the space. It was rumored to be the hangout of the band Garbage whenever they were in town, recording at SmartStudios. Try as I might, I never ran into them.

"Stoli martini, straight up with a twist," I said to the guy behind the bar. I was seated at the end, directly across from the copy of Garbage's platinum album. He saw me looking at it.

"You just missed them," he said putting ice in a cocktail shaker.

"Huh?" I said, confused and a little tipsy.

"Shirley and the boys. They just left." Of course they did. I sipped my cocktail in silence. I had truly struck out on all fronts.

Don't Hate the Playah (Memory #22)

Aaron and I were to meet at Pizzeria Uno, on Mineral Point Road, on Madison's west side. He asked if he could bring a friend on our first date, as he was new to gay dating. Whatever that meant. I should have smelled trouble, but desperation took hold and I agreed to it.

Aaron and his friend Todd were waiting for me in the vestibule. "Hi! I'm Aaron," he said, shaking my cold hand. It was only October, but it was freezing out.

"Hi," I said shaking Todd's hand. "Shall we eat?" I held the door for them and Todd told the hostess we needed a table for three. After placing our pizza order, I had to get it out of the way. "So, I have to ask, why the chaperone?" They both laughed.

"Well," Aaron began. "Until very recently, I was married."

"Oh," I said, things becoming clearer.

"The divorce was finalized two weeks ago. We have joint custody of our daughter." I was fascinated by this story. And I was incredibly attracted to him. Who knows? Maybe this little starter family could be mine? I thought.

"What's your daughter's name?" I asked somewhere between nervousness and curiosity.

"Ella."

"I love that name. So, how do the two of you know each other?" They looked at one another and laughed and their faces turned bright red.

"My wife caught me cheating on her with Todd." There was the other shoe. It dropped.

"Why aren't you two together?" They again laughed at my question.

"It was fun, but we really aren't suited to date," offered Todd.

"Todd was awesome at helping me come out and deal with everything. He has been a truly great friend." Their hands locked. I felt like I shouldn't be there, that I should have been at table by myself so they could be left alone. In my head, I vowed to never see either of them again. Just get through dinner, I thought.

In the parking lot, I said goodbye to them. They both hugged me. I watched them get into Aaron's bright red car and drive off. I fired up the Rabbit and headed back to my apartment. The whole exchange left me baffled and feeling off my axis.

I put the leftover pizza in my fridge and slipped into my pajamas. I turned on the modem and checked my email. Nothing from Aaron but, Todd had written me.

> *Kyle,*
>
> *I know this is going to sound weird,*
> *especially since you were there to meet*

Aaron, but I thought we had a connection
and I'd really like to go on a date with
you. Alone. I hope you'll say yes. I spoke
to Aaron and he is ok with this.

Todd

Now, I really was shocked, and intrigued. I knew that
Phaedra was planning on having a Halloween party at a
house she was housesitting for so I invited him to
that. He said yes.

On Halloween, we met in the Barnes & Noble parking
lot and he got into the Rabbit and headed off to the
party, neither of us in costume. I started making small
talk, as I was lost and trying to get back on the right
street.

"What is it that you do?" I asked while trying to find a
street sign.

"I sell wholesale office supplies to different accounts,
mainly in Janesville." That's where he lived.

"That's cool," I said, turning onto the correct
street. "There it is," I said noticing Phaedra's blue
minivan in the driveway. She always said she drove it
because she played the string bass and had two large
dogs. I secretly thought it was because she wanted to
be a mom.

"Kyle!" she said as she opened the front door, dressed
as a cop.

"Phaedra, this is Todd." They shook hands and we
walked in. I hated parties where I knew no one. I mean

I knew Phaedra and I kind of knew Todd. We made our way to the kitchen and helped ourselves to beer.

About a half hour later, Todd tells me that he rented a hotel room on the west side, near Target as he didn't feel like driving back to Janesville and assumed I didn't want to drive home either. We went and collected his vehicle and met at the Marriott.

Upon entering the room, we stripped out of our clothes and onto the bed closest to the bathroom. After having the most aggressive, animal-style sex, we fell asleep. In the morning, we quietly got ready without speaking. He waved goodbye to me without having kissed me or made plans for a second date. I thought this was weird and really hoped he didn't regret last night.

Back at my apartment, after I showered, I saw that Todd was in the same chat room as I. Aaron was in it as well.

> *Kyle: Thanks for last night.*

A few minutes passed and he wrote:

> *Todd: Can you believe that loser actually thought you and I weren't dating? Sex was good though. We should have had a three-way.*

It was clear this message was not intended for me. My lower eyelids were holding back tears. I shut my modem off without logging out and cried. Why were people so cruel? I thought.

Blinking Joseph
(Memory #23)

I climbed the stairs to Grandma's attic. When I moved to New York, that's where I stored all of my belongings. Over the years, I had shipped out most of the stuff to my New York apartment. I had sold off the larger pieces of furniture. All that remained now were a few books and a couple boxes of photographs. I opened an Armani cologne gift box Evan had given me and started to leaf through pictures: prom, class trip to France, my Milwaukee friends and I drinking. I closed the lid on those memories.

There it was. Sitting in the corner of the room. The Blinking Joseph. I set the box down and walked over to it, resting my hands on Joseph's plastic head.

Most of the time, when we were together, Anka and I were easily amused. I would pick her up (she never got her license) and we would head out in search of mischief. Usually, we'd end up in Platteville. We'd have dinner at Country Kitchen and then to K-Mart to ride the mechanical horses outside the entrance. One time, we got kicked out of Pizza Hut because I put five dollars' worth of quarters in the jukebox and selected only *Heaven Is a Place on Earth*. The manager eventually unplugged the machine and asked us to leave.

Driving back to my apartment, we passed through an even smaller town called Belmont. We're talking blink and you miss it small town. They had their usual holiday decorations up: garlands that stretched across the street, light pole to light pole. They lit up and spelled "Noel." This particular sign had two bulbs burnt out so it just said "No." We laughed so hard I almost hit a parked car.

"Oh, my God! Look at the blinking Joseph!" I pulled the car to a halt. Anka braced herself on the dash with her arms.

"That sounds like an Irish curse." She laughed at her own joke.

"Or a really bad cocktail. We HAVE to have it!" Sitting on the front yard of some festive house was a nativity scene. Not just any. Oh no. Each party member was made out of hollow plastic, with a light at the base. Everyone was there, the wise men, shepherds, angels, even sheep and camels. Oh, and of course, Mary, Jesus and Joseph. Except that Joseph was the only one with a blinking light.

"I'll be right back," Anka said in a determined voice. She sprinted across the highway and crouched down behind the nativity. With stealth precision, she unplugged Joseph, swept him up in her arms and darted back across the highway. With Joseph in the backseat, I tore off. We laughed the whole way back to my apartment. There, we displayed blinking Joseph in my deep windowsill for all to enjoy.

I ran my hand across Joseph's head, at the seam line, and wondered how that family ever replaced him. Poor Jesus, I thought, growing up without a father.

Toss Ya One
(Memory #24)

The ad read:

> *UW Business major, 23 years old, seeking LTR. Love field hockey, video games, and dining out. Am compassionate and a pretty funny guy. Must respond with a picture to get mine.*

Sounded good to me! I drafted a response (with requisite photo) and clicked send. To my surprise, a few minutes later, he wrote back. His name was Marvin. He attached his photo and he was really sexy. There's no other word for it than sexy. Jet-black hair, combed back, slightly olive skin, brown eyes so dark they looked black, full, beautiful lips and a great smile. I sighed. He saw *my* photo and wrote *me* back!

A few email exchanges later, we made plans to meet Saturday night for dinner. I looked at his photo again. I neglected to see the first time that he had hiked up his polo shirt to reveal his washboard abs. I pressed my hand against my stomach and suddenly felt very flabby. I mean, I wore size 32 pants so it's not exactly like I was Jabba The Hutt, but still.

The plan was to meet at Tutto Pasta, my usual spot for Italian food downtown Madison. I saw him standing outside with his hands in his pockets, wearing a long black trench coat. His face looked fuller than his photo. Must have used an old one, I thought. Still, he was beautiful.

"Marvin?" I asked as I approached him.

"Hey, Kyle," he said. "You ready to eat?"

"Let's do it," I said and held the door for him. The restaurant was packed. We managed to get a small table near the window. After our orders were placed (fettuccini alfredo for me, and shrimp scampi for him), that's when the real fun began.

"So," he started. "You work at Roads' End?"

"Yup. In the CAD department." It was easier than getting into the minutiae of what I did.

"And how do you like it." He sipped his Chianti.

"Fine. Fine. All good. What about you? How's school going?"

"Midterms are over. I'm happy with that." I noticed a big, shiny watch on his wrist. He held it out for me to see. "Rolex. Dad bought it for me for getting straight A's."

"Very nice." I didn't know what else to say.

"Things go well, I'll get a new BMW at the end of the year."

"What does your father do?"

"Investment banker." That made sense. "My family lives in Chicago."

"What's the prize after the BMW?" I asked playfully.

He smirked and said: "I get a condo." Seemed like the next logical step. I thought of my tiny studio apartment out in the sticks. "What kind of car do you drive?"

"Umm, a VW Rabbit." Thankfully, our food arrived.

"Uh huh," he said, taking a whole shrimp in his hands started to eat it. Use a fork, I thought. My pasta was so good that I was soon engrossed in my meal and not his lack of manners. My radar as to whether or not a date was going well was tuned to military grade precision. I knew this wasn't working out, so at least the food was delicious.

"So, you say you live in Mineral Point? I don't even know where that is," he said.

"It's forty-five minutes southwest of here on Highway 151." He nodded

"How do you live all the way out there?"

"Well, it's close to work and I don't mind the drive into Madison." Again, he just nodded.

The server set the check down in between us. He picked it up and glanced at the total. "I got this," he said with a cockiness that made me want to punch him. As if he were implying I couldn't afford the meal.

"Listen," he started. I wanted him to just shut up. "I'm guessing that it's not every day that you get to go on a date with someone as hot as me, much less sleep with one. So, I'm going to toss ya one."

"Excuse me?" I couldn't believe what I was hearing. Marvin, over the course of the meal had turned into Douchey McDoucherson. What was this bit about wanting a long-term relationship? And being funny and compassionate? He tapped my leg with his foot.

"You heard me. I'll toss you one." He tried to rub his foot up and down my leg.

"No thanks," I said as I stood up, grabbed my coat and ran for the door. Once in the safe haven of the Rabbit, I realized that I forgot to take the to-go container with my leftover pasta. Damn, I thought. Probably just as well, the fewer reminders of the evening the better.

The Easy Way Out
(Memory #25)

With my Mapquest printouts at the ready, I closed the door to the Rabbit and pulled out of my driveway. Several cassettes I had made of all my favorites songs were sitting in the console. I rolled down the windows and opened the moonroof.

I made my mind up that I was returning to college to study fashion design. But, I didn't know where. I did an exhaustive Internet search and discovered the UW system had a fashion program way, way up north in Menomonie at UW-Stout. I took a day off from work and made an appointment to meet with the dean and tour the department.

With Spice Girls in the tape deck, I started the four-hour car ride north. I stopped at Culver's along the way for lunch. Having devoured a butter burger and deep fried cheese curds, I continued on. I loved all the oversized fiberglass statues lining the truck stops along the way. I wish I had my camera on me, I thought.

Menomonie was a quaint town of about fifteen thousand residents. I'm sure more during the college season. It was close to Minneapolis, which is where Target is headquartered. I could do this, I thought. Or there was Roads' End after college. The idea of moving to New York for fashion school terrified me.

I pulled into the parking lot on campus and closed up the Rabbit. I grabbed my paperwork and headed into the building. It was summer and the school was out, save for a few classes here and there. It was too late for me to apply for the fall semester, but I wanted to make the best decision and pay off as much of my existing student loan debt before starting up again.

"Professor Rubin?" I asked the grey haired woman behind the desk. She was what I pictured Anna Wintour looking like at age 70.

"You must be Kyle. Pleased to meet you." I shook her hand. "Let's get started with the tour."

She led me through the various sewing rooms, explained the benefits of each piece of machinery, spoke about the internship programs they had with top companies around the country. I felt like a star football player being courted by a college team.

I thanked Professor Rubin and got back in my car. She waved at me as I drove out of the parking lot. I couldn't put my finger on, but something wasn't sitting right with me. I couldn't decide if it seemed too easy to attend UW-Stout over a school in New York. Or maybe it was I was being a snob and felt that I could only attend a prestigious school if I was ever going to get a decent job.

A thousand thoughts tumbled in my mind as I drove back to my apartment. What was I going to do? I didn't have to decide in that moment, but as the arguments circled, I always landed on New York. Ok. So, if it's New York, which school? I wanted to go to Parsons, but couldn't afford it. It was nearly double what F.I.T.'s tuition was.

The next day at lunchtime, I sat in the Corporate Sales

cafeteria by myself, still playing out a million scenarios in my mind. Adam heated up his leftover pizza and joined me.

"Dude, where were you yesterday?"

"I went to visit UW-Stout's fashion design program."

"Stout! Stout! The easy way out!" he chanted, mouth full of pizza. That was the final factor in my decision.

Straight as an Arrow
(Memory #26)

"Pat's Bar after work?" June asked, sticking her head around the corner. I nodded in agreement. "Great. I'll round up the troupes." Pat's was our new watering hole. Dodgeville's rotation of four bars stayed the same, taking up new ownership every six months to a year. The interiors and staff never changed. A new sign went up and that was it.

"You ready?" Adam asked as 3:30 P.M. approached.

"You know it," I said, filling out my time sheet. I packed up my CDs into my messenger bag and met the group by the front desk. One by one, we filed out to our cars and headed to the bar. It was the full group tonight. Should be fun, I thought.

Friday night in any small town across the country is filled with workers, celebrating the end of the week in dive bars, with cheap beer, smoke and laughter and complaints filling the air. We nestled into our usual spot and all placed our usual orders: different beers for everyone, martini for me. We each shared our various opinions on whatever corporate oppression we felt we were suffering under. Adam was sitting next to me.

"When was the last time that Greg joined us?" he whispered to me.

"I don't think ever."

"Yeah, that's bizarre. Whatever," I said, taking the last sip of my martini. The group continued to order drinks, everyone taking a turn buying a round. As it got closer to 9 P.M., the group started to break up. Soon it was just Adam, Greg and I. The three of us sat in awkward silence, drinking our beverages.

"Gentlemen," Adam announced, slurring his words a little. "It's time for me to go." He stood up, put his coat on and left. Greg and I sat there in silence. I bought him a drink. I figured, why not. It was the nice thing to do.

"Thank you," he said to me, taking the beer bottle from the bartender.

"No problem," I said. He slid over into the stool next to me that Adam had just occupied. I sipped my drink. His knee touched mine. I didn't move and neither did he. Then I felt his hand moving from his knee onto mine. I looked at him and he smiled a sly grin.

"You want to go out back to my car?" he asked. I nodded. We settled up the tab, left and rounded the corner to his Mustang parked behind the bar. There was a chill in the air. I was happy to get into the passenger side of his car.

I didn't know what to do. Moments earlier, I thought Greg was straight as could be. Catalog-cover, fit-model, every-girl-in-the-office-swooned-over, Greg. He leaned in and we started to kiss. He very gently held my head in his hands as we kissed. I expected him to be sloppy and clumsy. I ran my hands over his beautiful pecs as his hand slowly made its way up my thigh. He stopped just below my crotch.

Fog completely covered all the windows as we continued to make out. The intensity ratcheting up, he pulled back and sat facing the steering wheel. I thought he just needed a break and we would continue any moment.

"I can't do this," he said. "It's just the beers and the tension between us, I think, that's built to this. I'm sorry." He turned on the car and drove me one block over to the Rabbit. I got out of the car and he sped away. I didn't say a word about what happened. Neither did he.

You're Not My Type
(Memory #27)

I stared at the search field on the personals message board. What would I search for? What search term had eluded me, which kept me from meeting my boyfriend? I went through the usual suspects: funny, committed, monogamous, intelligent, and witty. What else? I typed *Mystery Science Theater 3000*. One ad appeared. It was for a guy my age named Hanson, who lived in Oshkosh, about three hours northeast from me.

His picture was beautiful. It was a moody, black and white photo of him in a graveyard, leaning on a gravestone with his arms folded. He had on the same rollneck sweater that I favored. He had thick curly hair and a stubble beard. From his stats, I learned that his hair was red. He had a thin, angular face with lots of freckles. He was working in the administrative offices of UW-Oshkosh.

I decided to write to him. A day later, he wrote me back. He said he was excited to find someone else who liked *MST3K* and we started emailing back and forth some of our favorite lines. It was all very light-hearted and playful. On Saturday night, when a new episode aired, I would imagine him sitting there next to me. Together, laughing at the same jokes. Afterwards, we would make love and fall asleep in each other's arms.

This playful banter lasted three weeks before we spoke on the phone. He had a very soft, delicate voice. It matched his photo perfectly. He said he liked my voice. We had so much in common. We both loved jazz, both drove VW's, both voted Democratic, both loved *MST3K*.

"Can I see your photo?" he asked on the phone one night. "I bet you're cute." He hadn't seen a photo of me. I answered his ad without sending one of myself.

"Ok," I said nervously.

"C'mon! It's just a matter of protocol at this point. We definitely have a ton in common. I'm sure you're beautiful."

His begging finally wore me down. I said I would send a picture of me as soon as we got off the phone. Back in the days of dialup, I couldn't send one while talking to him. We said goodnight and I logged into my email as promised. I flipped through my photos folder, in search of the best one of me. I hated them all. I decided on one taken recently at a party. I thought it pretty accurately portrayed me. Sent.

I waited for a response. I knew he would race to his computer upon hanging up so he could finally see me staring back at him. Nothing came. I waited. I opened a bottle of wine and waited some more. Finally, I wrote him to confirm that he received the photo. He wrote back:

> *Kyle,*
>
> *Sorry, you're just not my type.*
>
> *Regards,*
> *Hanson*

Some years later, I received an email from him out of nowhere. He wrote at length about how he had fallen in love with a Chinese exchange student, but they broke up and he could really use a friend, maybe call each other while watching an episode of *MST3K*. I clicked delete.

True Lies
(Memory #28)

I woke up early on Saturday, not being able to sleep. Frustrated by this, I made coffee and logged into my email. While all this was happening, I turned up the dial on my thermostat and rummaged for my slippers. They had a way of never being in the same spot twice.

Coffee in hand, I looked at my inbox. The usual credit card and male enhancement pill offers removed, I saw an email from my friend Jill. I had hung out with her occasionally since moving back.

> *K,*
> *You need to meet Truman at Dick's. He works there, is our age, and just came out! Apparently, he told the butcher department that he's gay.*
> *J*

Hmmm. A real, live gay person, working and living in the area? And his name was Truman? I went and took stock of my fridge and cupboards and put together a shopping list. That way, if he weren't working, the trip wouldn't be for nothing. I could always swing by Walmart and get fabric.

I showered and got dressed and went out to the Rabbit. There was a crust of frost across the windshield. It took about five minutes to clear it. I shivered as I got into the warm car and set off for Dick's over in Dodgeville.

I parked the car as close as I could to the entrance and ran into the warmth of the store. I grabbed a cart and started peacefully walking up and down each aisle, slowly so I could run into Truman. I made it through the entire store with no sign of him. I decided to check out and go home.

After putting away the groceries, I slipped back into my pajamas and turned on the modem. There was another email from Jill.

> *K,*
> *Scratch that. Truman just told the guys to*
> *get a rise out of them and see their*
> *reaction. He's got a girlfriend, I*
> *think. Sorry! Wanna do dinner soon?*
> *J*

I sighed. I knew it. It was too good to be true. I turned off the computer and went over to the piano and played Mozart. I played for about a half hour but it didn't calm me down as it usually does. I went back to the computer and typed up an email to Jill.

> *J,*
> *I know this is not directed at you, but tell*
> *Truman that's a terrible joke to play on*
> *someone. Especially when I'm so lonely*
> *and it's so difficult to meet anyone here that*
> *it got my hopes up for nothing. Tell him*
> *that his actions have consequences.*
> *K*

And I hit send. I was really worked up. I grabbed my favorite blanket and curled up on my chair and watched

Mystery Science Theatre 3000. Even that produced a
lukewarm response at best. Why was this getting under
my skin? Getting up to preheat the oven for tonight's
pizza, I checked my mail again.

> *K,*
> *You can tell him yourself. He's coming*
> *over for dinner tonight. You're*
> *invited. Bring wine.*
> *J*

I shut off the oven. Maybe, that's what I needed, a
face-to-face confrontation to purge this feeling in me. I
jumped in the shower and picked out my outfit, my
favorite navy rollneck sweater from J.Crew and chinos
and my new felt clogs. I know. Don't judge. I was,
am and always will be a fan of easy on, easy off. In so
many respects.

I grabbed the lone bottle of wine that hadn't been
consumed from my counter and headed out. Jill lived
with her boyfriend Scott in an apartment two blocks
down on High Street. I knocked on the door.

"Hi, Scott," I said, as he opened the door.

"Kyle! Great to see you," he said, stepping aside so I
could get inside and warmed up. I took off my coat and
set it on the coat rack behind the door. They had
essentially the same apartment I did, except they had a
separate bedroom. I was jealous.

"Kyle, this is Truman," said Jill. Truman was sitting on
a stool at their work island with his back to the
door. He turned and I melted. He was beautiful,
shorter than me, wiry, wavy brown hair, deep mocha

colored eyes, and the sexiest stubble beard.

"I'm Truman. I heard you want to tell me something," he said, shaking my hand.

"Um," I fumbled, not thinking the topic would be the first one we spoke about. "Yes. Yes! Actually, I do. I think you think you were being funny, trying to get a reaction from those guys, but do you have any idea how isolating it feels to be gay and live here? Why didn't you tell them you were Jewish? Or from the Ukraine?" I was getting worked up.

"Sorry." I didn't react. "I truly am. Please forgive me." He extended his hand again and I shook it. His face was so adorable; I couldn't stay agitated for long.

"There. That's out of the way. Now, let's eat," said Jill, setting a big bowl of spaghetti onto the work island, which doubled as dining table. I pulled up the stool next to Truman and offered the group a glass of wine. Jill handed me a corkscrew.

Dinner was quite pleasant. It was much better than my frozen pizza. And the conversation was good. Truman was taking time off from school to figure out what was next. That's what I told people, too. He was very interested in painting. That's what he was doing when he wasn't bagging groceries at Dick's. After dinner, Scott put *Monty Python's The Meaning of Life* into the VCR while Jill and I cleaned up. When we were done, we joined Truman and Scott on the sofa. Jill only made it half way into the film and that's when I excused myself and walked the two blocks back home.

I turned the heat back up. After receiving my first

winter heating bill, I became very aware of the temperature setting when I wasn't there. Out of habit, I turned on the modem and poured a glass of vodka. Just as I was going to sit at my computer, there was a knock at the door. I stood frozen, not wanting to move. Who was there so late at night? I had the lights on so it was obvious that I was home. A second round of knocks came. Slowly I opened the door.

"Kyle, you mind if I come in?" It was Truman. I opened the door the rest of the way.

"Sure," I said

"Nice pajamas," he said as I quickly closed the door. Not wanting any of my precious and expensive heat escaping.

"Thanks," I said, knowing it wasn't a compliment. I offered him a drink as he sat on the futon.

"Sure," he said, looking around my apartment. "Nice place."

"Thanks. Where are you staying?" I asked while pouring a second glass of vodka and handing it to him.

"With my folks." I sat next to him on the futon. I leaned over and turned the stereo on. Stan Getz was first up in the disc changer. "But not for long. I'm planning on returning to college soon."

I sipped my vodka.

"What's with all the dresses? Are you a tranny?"

I choked on my drink. "No. I am really into design. I've been teaching myself how to sew. Those are my practice creations."

"Gotcha. That's cool." We spoke about holiday plans, jazz, where to get the best burger in Madison, our favorite *Monty Python* lines. I wanted to be asleep by now, but it was fun making a new friend. At least something positive came from all of this, I thought. "Listen, what are your New Year's plans?"

"You're pretty much looking at it," I said.

"Mind if I come over? I mean, I don't have any plans and I thought maybe we could have a movie marathon and make dinner."

"I'd like that." Truman set his glass on the kitchen table and put on his coat. I wished him well, put the glass in the sink, brushed my teeth and crawled onto the futon and pulled the blanket over me. The futon smelled like him, a Calvin Klein cologne I couldn't name, but somehow knew.

Over the next few weeks, I didn't think much of Truman really. My mom had given me a serger for Christmas and I had taken to learning how to sew knitted fabrics. Knits were not my strong suit. That was apparent.

New Year's Eve was soon upon me. I tidied up the apartment and put away all of my sewing equipment, watered the plant and checked my email. Truman confirmed he was coming over. We were going to watch a bunch of James Bond films and he was bringing Chinese food from Dick's, that and a ton of booze.

"Kyle! Happy New Year!" Truman said, entering my apartment and handing me several bags that clinked when they hit each other. He set up a little Chinese buffet on the kitchen counter while I got the first movie ready: *Diamonds Are Forever*. We each fixed a plate and I made us martinis and sat on the futon. Next up were *A View To A Kill* and more martinis. Followed by *Dr. No* and even more martinis.

We paused the movie to watch the countdown to the New Year. Striking midnight, we clinked our glasses together.

"I'll be right back," he said with a grin and closed the bathroom door. Being tipsy, I thought it would be funny to play U2's *New Year's Day*. I found the disc and put it in the player. About thirty seconds into the song, Truman returned, completely naked.

"Umm," I said, not sure of what to do or say.

"Now you! Let's see it."

"What? We're comparing sizes here?" I knew I had him beat. He nodded and stared at my crotch. It was then I noticed he was completely hard. I figured I would oblige him. I stood up and slowly took off my t-shirt, unbuttoned my jeans and slipped them and my boxers off together.

"We need to compare them when they are both hard," he said, walking over to me and taking mine in his hands and stroking it slowly. Mine was already bigger than his erect one. He leaned in and kissed my cheek. He came back and we were then lip-locked. He was an ok kisser, I thought. Moments later, I was on the floor, on all fours with him entering me from behind, Bono still singing to us.

After we were done, we both laid on my floor, facing the ceiling. "What the hell just happened?" I asked, out of breath.

"I think it was pretty obvious."

"No, I mean, that whole 'I'm straight' thing."

"I guess I'm bi." I offered him a towel as he started to dress. I cleaned myself off and got into my pajamas. I offered him the remainder of the food and drink that he had brought. He told me to keep it. He kissed me on the cheek and left.

I never saw Truman again. Not that I really wanted to. Last I heard, he had finally come out of the closet and was dating someone. Good for him. At least the first few moments of the New Year were spent getting laid.

Exhaustion
(Memory #29)

I waved goodbye to June and Mona as we left the
bar. It was Thursday night. We had a particularly
trying day at work, the kind that can only be repaired by
venting over alcohol. I put the key in the ignition of the
Rabbit and turned it on. A loud, howling grumble came
from underneath the car. Did I need to change the
oil? Should I upgrade to the premium gasoline? No,
this was a muffler issue, I thought.

I exited the parking lot and headed down Main Street
towards the exit for the highway to return to my
apartment. With each shift of the gear, the sound got
louder and louder. I was now very self-conscious of it,
not wanting to draw any attention to my sad little car.

The next morning I got in it and hoped that overnight
she was repaired. Maybe it was a fluke thing,
something she needed to get out of her system. She just
needed a good night's sleep. I turned the car on and
again she grumbled and growled.

Pulling into the parking lot at Roads' End, I could see
Adam stopped just outside his car. I parked next to
him.

"Man, you need to get a new muffler," he said.

"I know! I'm already embarrassed." It was incredibly
embarrassing. People would turn their heads as I
passed them on the highway or pulled up next to them
at the stoplight. I called my stepfather and asked if he
could take a look at it after work. He agreed.

Around 4 P.M., I headed out towards my mom and stepfather's farm. I couldn't tell if it was me but the car seemed to be getting louder. To the point where it was unbearable and the radio did nothing to mask it.

"Holy shit," Mom said as I shut off the car. "I could hear you a mile away."

"Ok. That's being dramatic." My stepfather asked to bring the car up to the machine shed. There, he put it up on ramps and made his inspection. Sure enough, there was a giant hole in the muffler. The entire exhaust system, in fact, was rusted. He said it would all have to be replaced, but he thought he could weld a piece of metal over the muffler to help silence it a little.

He started the car after he was finished putting the welding tools away. It did help, probably canceled out the noise by half. I couldn't thank him enough. I got in and headed towards Madison for a night out. The car was loud, but not like it was. I thought, before I had dinner, I would go and price out a new exhaust system. Couldn't be any more than $100, I thought.

Just outside Verona, the exhaust seemed to backfire and cough a little. I slowed down slightly and looked in the rear view mirror. All of a sudden, a giant *CLANG* rang out and the entire exhaust system dropped out from underneath the car. The car behind me had to swerve into the left lane to avoid hitting it. I watched as the muffler and pipes jumped down the highway and landed on the shoulder. The car was now deafening. I had never in my life heard something so loud. The loudest motorcycle had nothing on the Rabbit.

Immediately, I turned off the highway and took back roads into Madison. I went straight to Midas on University Avenue.

"Yup. Your exhaust is gone," said the mechanic. Seriously? I thought.

"Is there anything you can do in the short term? A patch up job?" I begged.

"Nope. You're going to need a full replacement."

"How long will that take?"

"Well, I have to special order the parts. We don't stock anything for this model."

"Ok, how long will that take?"

"About a week," he said. My face dropped. The thought of having to drive with that sound for a week made me sick to my stomach.

"And how much is it going to cost?" He flipped through a giant book that had type the size of a phone book. His grease covered finger sliding along to find the Rabbit.

"For the new system, for what you need, is going to be $800." I almost fainted. What was I going to do? I needed a car. The car needed an exhaust system, so I put down a deposit and told him to go ahead and special order the parts.

My $100 car with its $800 transmission and now $800 exhaust system was a $1,700 car. Not wanting even more people to look at my car and point, I turned around and went back to my apartment. There, I hid out until I received the call that the parts were in.

Greasy
(Memory #30)

Adam approached my cube with a grin on his face. I could tell he was up to something. He looked like a little kid. I busted out laughing before he could even speak.

"What?" he said.

"You're up to something," I said.

"What makes you say that?"

"You have your mischievous face on." He laughed at me. "Spill it."

"Ok. So you know how the scanner at my desk shit the bed?" I loved his use of the English language.

"Yes."

"Well, I put in a request for I.T. to come and fix it. And they did this morning."

"Ok…" I said, hoping this was heading somewhere quickly.

"So, this guy named Tyler came and replaced it. And I got you a date." I choked on my coffee. "Yup. You can thank me later."

"What? How?" I was confused, mortified and excited all at once.

"I could tell he was gay. So, I asked him if he was single and he said yes so I brought him over and pointed you out to him and asked if he'd like to go on a date with you and he said yes. Here's his information." Adam handed me a piece of paper. On it was Tyler's personal email and phone number.

"I can't believe you did that. What does he look like?"

"Check him out on the Intranet." Adam pointed to my screen. I forgot the company had just rolled out a new directory, which included a photo of all employees. I think I blocked it out more than forgot, thinking of my picture with one eye lid more closed than the other and my bedhead. I looked like I just came off a bender. Maybe I did.

I found Tyler's photo. He was really cute, bright red wavy hair and beard, freckled face and the most adorable smile. "That's him?" I asked Adam for confirmation. He nodded. "But, he's hot. Are you sure you pointed me out and not Greg?"

"No, I said, that guy with glasses. Greg doesn't wear glasses." Adam slugged me in the shoulder as if saying, go, get 'em! I wrote Tyler an email introducing myself and apologizing for Adam's forwardness. I clicked send and sat back and smiled. This day sure turned around quickly, I thought.

> *Kyle,*
> *Don't be silly! I'm glad Adam pointed you out. You're very cute! When is good to meet? My schedule is a little crazy as I'm starring in a musical after work at UW-*

Platteville for the next six weeks.
Tyler

I wrote back that my schedule was like his 7 A.M. to 3:30 P.M. and that I lived in Mineral Point. He could easily swing by before or after his rehearsals, as he had to drive through town to get to Platteville. He wrote back and asked if he could swing by after work and we could meet and hangout for a bit.

After work, I raced to my apartment to tidy up before he arrived. He got there not long after I did. I nervously opened the door and welcomed him in. I had *The Simpsons* on the T.V.

"Kyle!" he said, coming in for a hug. Very forward, I thought, but wrapped my arms around him. He kissed the side of my neck. I was instantly hard. I could feel his solid pecs pressing into my chest.

"Can I get you anything?" I asked, stepping back from the embrace.

"No. Just you." He flopped on the futon. Not sitting, but lying down and propped up on one arm. He tapped the edge of the futon for me to join him. I moved in next to him, our erections pressing into one another as we made out. This guy waits for nothing, I thought. I started to unbutton his shirt. He stopped me with his hand.

"Is everything ok?" I asked, coming up for air.

"I can't. Don't have the time. I have to get to rehearsal." He stood up. I could see the outline of his erection under his chinos. He looked at mine. He came in for another kiss.

"You want to come back after?" I asked, hoping to pick up where we were leaving off.

"I can't. We're all going out after rehearsal. I'll email you. Hey, do you want to come to a performance? I can comp you a ticket." I said yes and watched him leave the apartment.

A couple days later, I got an email from him saying that Friday night's performance of *Grease* was the opening and he left a ticket at the box office for me. I was excited to have plans. I was excited to see him again. Maybe I could see him after, I thought.

Friday night, I made my way through the auditorium to my assigned seat. I had no issue going to things alone. I was kind of used to it. I was not about to stay at home and miss a movie or concert or meal just because I didn't have a date. The production was very low budget and cheesy and the acting and singing was just ok. Tyler was actually quite good. *Grease* was never my favorite musical, but this sure beat a frozen pizza and video rental.

After the show, I went back to the lobby as the cast flooded out to meet their friends and families and receive accolades. I looked for Tyler, but couldn't find him. Group by group, the lobby thinned out. It was clear that Tyler was not there. I walked back to the Rabbit and drove home. I emailed him that he was great and if he got this message and wanted to stop by my place, he could. I fell asleep in my chair waiting for him.

Monday morning, Adam approached my cube with the same grin. "So?" he asked, wanting me to spill the details about how I slept with Tyler over the weekend.

"Nada," I said, shaking my head. I saw an email come through from Tyler. He thanked me for the kisses and coming to the performance, but a fellow cast mate asked him out and he said yes. *You're The One That I Want* played in my head. I guess I wasn't the one.

No Call, No Show
(Memory #31)

"You've got a glow about you," said June as we sat around the break room table.

"I'm meeting him tonight," I said, giddy as I could possibly be.

"I worry about you meeting these men on the computer," offered Mona.

"I'll be fine!" We finished our coffees and headed back upstairs to the CAD area. I couldn't focus on the work in front of me. My mind wouldn't stop playing out how tonight would go. I would leave work promptly at 3:30 P.M., head to my apartment, shower, put out fresh flowers (which I would clip from the tiger lilies growing behind my apartment,) and light candles in each of the windows and on the table. And then, I would wait for him to arrive.

Him = Ian. We met online through a personals message board. We exchanged photos and I found him wildly attractive. He had blond hair, almost platinum, baby doll face, chocolate brown eyes and washboard abs. He felt compelled to send me that photo. I guess, if I looked like that, I would head straight to Glamor Shots and take a thousand shirtless photos. I stopped to think of me shirtless, in a cowboy hat and chaps and I busted out laughing.

Ian worked in P.R., crisis management, to be exact. I couldn't fathom his work, or ever being in a situation where I needed someone to manage my crisis. He was cocky and self-assured and there was something sexy about that. We emailed each other back and forth every day for three months. We would have met sooner, but he was in Ohio and I in Wisconsin.

Every night after work, I would rush home and turn my modem on, listening to the dings and the pings and screeches, anticipating having an email waiting there from him. And I always did. On a few occasions, we even spoke on the phone. He always called me, knowing that I didn't have a ton of money for long distance calls.

I printed his photo, ear-to-ear grin on his face, and carried it with me throughout my day. If I was feeling bored or melancholy, I would pull it from my pocket and look at it. In the off chance, I forgot about it on laundry day, I would print a fresh copy to replace it. Sometimes, while sitting at my work desk, clicking my mouse away, I dreamt of him proposing to me and whisking me off to Ohio where I would be his housewife. I would make sure our house was clean and full of fresh cut white tulips and Ella Fitzgerald on the stereo. I sighed.

> *Ian,*
> *I can't wait to see you tonight! Finally!*
> *Kyle*

I clicked send and sighed again. I fluffed the pillows on the futon, uncorked a bottle of merlot, loaded up the disc changer with Ella, and lit the candles. I cracked the blinds ever so slightly so I could make out if anyone was coming up to my door. I grabbed my kitchen shears and stepped outside and snipped some flowers. I hummed along to *Where or When* as I filled a vase with water and put the flowers on my kitchen table. The stage was set.

I realized that Ian would be in the car and on his way to see me without any way of checking his email. I poured a glass of wine and flopped down in my favorite chair. I kept the cordless phone next to me, in case he called with an update.

I poured another glass of wine. And another. And another. I realized I had polished off the bottle. The clock on the microwave read 9:41 P.M. Ian said he would be to my house by 8. Maybe he had car trouble? Stopped along the way to eat and lost track of time? I logged back into my email account to see if he emailed. Nothing. I opened another bottle of wine and sat back in my chair.

Around 3 A.M., I woke up, still in my chair. The tealights had long extinguished themselves. I looked around my apartment for Ian, thinking maybe he had arrived while I was drunk. No Ian. I opened my front door, thinking he would have left a note on the door if I slept through his arrival. No note. I logged back into my email. No email. I curled up in a ball on my futon and cried myself back to sleep. I never heard from Ian again.

Can You Hear Me Now?
(Memory #32)

Darren was short and nerdy, which was totally hot to me. He had black wiry hair cut very short, brown eyes the color of chocolate frosting and a smile that made me melt. He was studying law at the UW. We met online (naturally) and had agreed to meet after a month of chatting.

It was Saturday morning and it was already pushing 90 degrees. I loathed the summer. I wasn't one of those people who craved the heat. Wisconsin summers can be brutally humid and this one was no exception. I slathered on deodorant, pulled my polo shirt on, grabbed my car keys and headed out the door.

The Rabbit did not have air conditioning. I take that back, it did have it. It just didn't work. I was relegated to having the windows down and the moonroof open. After a while, I kind of got used to it. I would shake my head at the A/C dial staring at me, taunting me as I stuck to the faux leather seat.

Our meeting spot was by the Memorial Library on the UW campus. I parked in my usual spot in the parking garage on North Lake Street. I could see him standing on the corner as I exited the garage. He looked better than his photo and I was suddenly nervous I wouldn't live up to mine.

"Darren!" I said as I approached him.

"Hi Kyle," he said, hugging me. I felt a bolt of

electricity run through me. This was going to be dangerous.

"So great to meet you!"

"Likewise." We found a bench and sat down. "I can't believe this heat," he said.

"I know."

We made small talk for about fifteen minutes. I could tell there was chemistry between us, but at the same time, I knew that we wouldn't end up together. Call it a sixth sense or whatever, but I knew that we weren't going to have a second date.

"You want to do it?" he asked, just throwing it out there. I smiled.

"Sure," I said. "Want to go back to your place?"

"Can't. My roommates are all there."

"What are we going to do then?"

He stood up. "C'mon. We'll find a place." We started walking on the lakeshore path by Lake Mendota, through the Muir Woods. On our walk, we scouted for a place for our hookup. After a passerby had cleared us, he would rub my back or touch my ass, trying to get a feel for what was to come.

"This isn't looking good," I said, feeling defeated. Here was this totally hot guy who wanted to have sex with me and the only thing standing in our way was a location. I wasn't about to drive him back to

Mineral Point, sleep with him and drive him back to Madison.

"We'll find a place," he said, self-assured.

We continued to wander through the woods. I would have suggested the woods, but there were too many people out and about, jogging, wandering. I wondered if the people we passed were looking for a place like we were.

"There," I said, proudly pointing to a building with an open door. Darren followed me over to it and we quietly entered. "Let's see if there's anyone in here," I whispered to him. He was grinning.

We walked down the hallway, classroom after classroom, looking for someone who would tell us to leave. When we saw that the place was deserted, we went to a classroom at the end of the hall. Inside, I took a desk chair and wedged it under the doorknob so that if someone were to try and enter, we'd have time to get our clothes on. I also noticed an open window. We could exit that way, I thought.

Darren came up and wrapped his arms around me. His hands slid under my polo shirt and I was self-conscious of my sweaty back. I did the same to him and got the same result. I could feel his hard-on pressed into mine. He pulled me even closer as we started to kiss. He was a great kisser.

We stood there for what seemed like forever, just holding and kissing one another. He was so gentle and passionate. I wasn't expecting that as he came across as cocky and almost antagonistic during our chats. He pulled my polo shirt off and I did the same to him. I loved this dark, wiry chest hair. I ran my hands across it as he slipped one down the back of my pants.

"Let's lie down," he said. The second I was on my back, he was taking off my chinos. "Very nice." He took his jeans off.

"You too," I said, taking him in my hand. He crawled on top of me and kissed my neck. My eyelids grew heavy and I could barely make out the ceiling tiles above me. Softly, I caressed his back as he continued to kiss me.

"Wow," he said, flopping on his back after we were finished. We both were on our backs, staring up. His hand found mine. "That was incredible." It was. Maybe it was the location, maybe it was him, I don't know, but it was amazing.

We dressed in silence. I inspected the door. No one had tried to disturb us. Slowly, I opened it and peered down the hallway, no one in sight. We slipped out of the building as quickly as we had entered it.

"What is this place anyway?" I said outside, trying to determine our location.

"It's the school for the deaf," he said, pointing to the sign by the door. How did I miss that? Suddenly, I felt really guilty for having sex in that classroom, really great sex. Darren laughed. It was kind of funny in a weird, absurd way.

He kissed my cheek outside the parking garage. I was going to ask if he wanted to get something to eat, but we both needed showers. That and I knew that was it for us. I didn't write him again until about six months later when I was craving a repeat performance. He never wrote me back.

Just Friends
(Memory #33)

My Saturday morning consisted of making coffee and toast, checking my email and sewing. I was working on my version of the little black dress. Black satin, spaghetti straps, fitted top and flared at the waist ever so slightly. I was pleased with my work.

Mid-afternoon, I took a break to make a sandwich and check my email again. I had a response to my personal ad! I had the ad out there for several weeks with not one single response. I even edited it twice to catch some bites. Nothing.

> *Hello!*
>
> *My name is Mitchell. I admit that I am outside of your age requirements (I'm 39), but I live in Spring Green, your ad sounded sincere and I could use a new friend in the area. I love music, dining out, movies. The typical stuff. Hope to hear from you.*
>
> *Best,*
> *Mitchell*

Initially, I was bummed that it was a friendship response and not a romantic one. But, the more I thought about it, I didn't have many friends, much less any gay ones. I wasn't in a position to be turning away anyone. So, I responded that I would love to meet him for coffee whenever he was free. To my surprise, he wrote me right back and we planned to meet that night for dinner and coffee at the café a couple of blocks away from my apartment.

"Hi Regina," I said to the woman behind the counter as I entered The Grey Dog Café. It got its name from the grey stone pointer dog that hung above the front door. Regina was a middle-aged woman, with too many teeth for her mouth, who ran the café for a gay couple who lived in Chicago. She lived in the apartment above. She was always working every time I visited, without fail.

"Kyle! So great to see you," she said, retying her navy blue apron. "What'll it be?"

"Just a coffee for now. I'm meeting someone here for dinner."

"Ooooooh!" she teased.

"No. I wish. It's a guy who answered my personal ad looking for a friend. Besides, he's so much older than I am." She handed me the coffee.

"Well, friends are good!"

"Yeah, I know." I took a seat across from the counter. I was the only person in there. Not unusual for a Saturday night when most people in town were glued to their television sets. I sipped my coffee and watched the cars drive up and down High Street. Regina regaled me with stories from her week, who had come in and what they ordered and such. It was terribly boring, but it was all she had so I indulged her.

The door opened and the little bell at the top of it

announced another patron. A handsome, tall, trim guy with salt and pepper hair and black-framed glasses entered. He was really well dressed, I thought.

"Are you Kyle?" he asked as he approached.

"Yes! You must be Mitchell." We hugged. I offered him to sit down and a coffee, which he accepted. I introduced him to Regina who seemed to have an instant crush on him. Oh, Regina, I thought. Always betting on the wrong horse.

"What is good here?" he asked, looking over the menu.

"The roast beef sandwich is incredible."

"I'm a vegetarian." I felt embarrassed for having suggested meat.

"The very veggie salad is equally incredible." That's what he ordered. I went for the roast beef sandwich. "So, what is it that you do?" I asked.

"I run a furniture company with my dad. We make wooden mission style furniture."

"Wow! That's amazing. How did you get into that line of work?"

"Well, I grew up in California. I was born here, but we moved there when I was two. I had a whole career as a personal shopper in Beverly Hills for most of my life. It was only a few years ago that I suggested that Dad and I start a business. He is a master carpenter and I could sell."

"That really is amazing." I was mesmerized by his story. Taking something, a single idea and blowing it up into a business.

"It was just me, carting around samples in my car and Dad making the production pieces from his basement. Today, we have twenty employees."

"Wow." Our food arrived and we started eating. Throughout dinner, Mitchell told me crazy stories about his romantic life in L.A. He made me look like a prude. I laughed at his stories, as did Regina who was listening in. At closing time, we settled up the check and I walked Mitchell to his car. I hugged him goodbye and said we definitely needed to hang out again. He agreed.

The following week, I got an email from him, inviting me over to his house in Spring Green. He had bought a house there that was designed by a student of Frank Lloyd Wright. Coming from somewhat of an architecture background, I was eager to see the house.

Spring Green is twenty minutes north of Mineral Point. It is settled on the Wisconsin River, which connects eventually to the Mississippi River. It has the most verdant hillsides of the state. Everything is so intensely green in the spring and summer. It was also where Frank Lloyd Wright built his hillside home and architecture school named Taliesin, having fallen in love with the land.

I had driven by the school and house a thousand times. I imaged the stories that took place behind those walls. I even toured Taliesin to see if I wanted to attend school there and be a part of Wright's legacy. I decided against it for a more traditional path.

I crossed the bridge over the Wisconsin River and made my way into Spring Green. Finding Mitchell's house was easy. It was very clearly not like the neighboring ones. Most had the typical white siding and black shingles and dormers on the roof. Mitchell's house had sleek lines, tan bricks and maroon colored accents. He also didn't have the traditional grassy front lawn. Instead, it was abloom with dozens, if not hundreds of varieties of wild flowers. It was so beautiful.

"Kyle! Come on in." He gave me a tour of the space and pointed out which pieces of furniture were from his factory and which were estate sale finds. He then handed me an ice-cold gin martini.

"What do you want to do tonight?" I asked, sipping the martini carefully as to not spill.

"Do you feel like going to Madison? We could go shopping and have dinner."

"Sure, why not?" We finished our martinis and got into his brand new Volvo station wagon. He told me that the car was perfect for moving around samples. As he curved and wound through the back roads to Madison, we listened to big band music and traded stories from our dating lives. It was nice to have a new friend, I thought.

In Madison, we pulled into the parking lot of Goodwill. I looked at Mitchell as we exited the vehicle with a look that said, seriously?

"Hey! Don't knock it! You can find some real treasures here."

"Ok!" I said, keeping an open mind. We wandered up and down the aisles, making fun of their offerings. I did manage to find this cream colored, fitted polyester military style jacket. It was really campy. I loved it. I also found a vintage stainless steel desk chair and a bust of Beethoven to place on top of my piano. Mitchell got a set of highball glasses and a pair of plaid pants.

After hitting up a couple more thrift stores, we headed downtown to Restaurant Magnus, a new restaurant that had opened recently and I wanted to try. We were seated in the dining room and I had a perfect view of the jazz band in the bar area.

I ordered the steak and Mitchell the salmon. We both had a martini and then wine with dinner. He pressed me about my design school ambitions and we talked shop for a while. I pressed on about his dating life.

"It's been difficult. I have been out of a long-term relationship for about a year now. That's been the hardest thing I've ever done." That made me sad and wished that he and his boyfriend were back together. He then confided that the reason for the split was they both tested positive for HIV. I had suspected that Mitchell might be positive after hearing all the wild and crazy sex stories. I couldn't imagine what he was going through. I saw now why he needed and wanted a friend.

After dinner, we walked over the Café Montmartre and had more martinis before heading home. I hugged Mitchell goodnight and loaded my thrift store finds into the Rabbit as I thanked him for a wonderful night.

Mitchell became one of my biggest champions of my design ambitions. Every few weeks, we'd meet up at his house, he would review my sketches and designs and we'd head into Madison for vintage store shopping and dinner and drinks. Always at Restaurant Magnus and Café Montmartre. It felt good to have a friend.

Whatever Floats Your Boat
(Memory #34)

It had been forever since I had gotten laid. And I needed it. Badly. I met Craig online and we decided to meet in the Target parking lot. He said he would be wearing an evergreen colored puffer coat and grey fur trapper hat. There was no way I wouldn't be able to pick him out of the crowd. And there he was, leaning up against a rusting, old yellow station wagon.

"Hey, Kyle," he said recognizing me.

"Hi," I responded, shaking his cold hand. "So, should we go to your place?"

"Roommates are there."

"My place is forty-five minutes away. What are we doing to do?" I could see the outline of his penis under his jeans. I wanted him. "Is there any place we can go?"

He thought for a minute and tapped the side of his car with his hand. "Let's go," he said. I got in the passenger side of the car.

"Do you know a place out of the way?"

"We'll find one." We headed north on Junction Road into Middleton. We drove up and down streets, trying to find a dead end or a quiet, dark parking spot. Craig put his hand on my thigh and worked it up to my crotch. I was relieved. I mean, we were headed to do this, but I didn't have final confirmation he was into me.

"There," I said, pointing to a dark, dead end street. We parked and got out of the car. He put the seats down and we climbed in. I was on my back and he leaned in and started kissing me. He was such a good kisser. I loved the taste of him. I could see fog collecting on the windows. I was glad he left the heat on. He slowly unzipped my jeans and slid them down off of me, not stopping our make out session.

I pulled him up on top of me and we continued kissing. I slid my hands in between his jeans and underwear. I stopped my hand as if it touched something hot. His underwear was silky. He flopped over next to me and unbuttoned his jeans and slid them off. There was his beautiful penis, sitting erect beneath a lavender colored pair of women's silk panties. I tugged on the lace waistband.

"They are so much more comfortable," he explained. I slid them off as quickly as I could. This was a night of firsts. Sex in a car. Sex with a guy in panties. And sex in a car with a guy in panties.

Film Buff
(Memory #35)

"Are you Kyle?" asked a very unassuming guy with a soft voice.

"I am," I confirmed, standing to shake his hand. In front of me was Matt, my date.

"So great to meet you!" he said while sitting at the chair across from me. I could tell he liked me.

"Likewise! Do you want anything to drink?" Starbucks was hardly an original first date, but we couldn't think of anywhere else to go.

"Yes. What was I thinking? I'll be right back."

I studied him while he was waiting in line for his Grande Soy Latte. He was my height, spiky blond hair, black-framed glasses and smooth, porcelain skin. I bet he never has a five o'clock shadow, I thought. He was wearing a navy gingham dress shirt and light tan chinos. I could tell he dressed up for the occasion. These were not his normal clothes. I, too, dressed up, almost in the exact same outfit. We laughed about this as he sat back down.

"Tell me about your studies," I asked. Matt was getting his graduate degree in Film Studies. I told him that I was a huge David Lynch fan, but had never seen *Eraserhead*. He happened to have a copy and it was decided that I would have to watch it with him. We spoke about my love of Edith Head's design and how she inspired much of the clothing I made. Being with him was effortless.

We took our coffees and made our way to Lake Mendota. The Union Terrace was packed so we walked way past it to an open pier to sit on. We laughed and joked around for close to an hour. It felt like we had known each other our whole lives, or at least for a very long period of time. He demanded that we meet again. I couldn't say no.

The following week, he took me to his favorite Chinese restaurant. Not the typical "date" restaurant, but the food was out of this world good. He asked if I wanted to take him up on that offer to see *Eraserhead*. I said yes. I didn't have to work the next day and I really wanted to see the film.

Matt had a studio apartment on North Bedford, near the U-Haul office. I was excited to see where he lived. I got to see a lot of apartments since no one ever wanted to drive forty-five minutes to see mine. It was your garden-variety studio apartment, but smelled like oranges. I liked that. He had a welcome mat outside his front door that said: "Hi! I'm Mat," a gift from his father.

"Make yourself at home," he said. "I need to use the bathroom." I went straight for the photos hanging above his futon. In neatly matted frames, were a dozen vintage images of naked men. I was a little put off by this, but at least they were vintage. That somehow made it more acceptable. I wandered over to his desk by the window and saw a stack of gay porno magazines and a stack of DVDs with men in various intimate positions.

I wandered over to the kitchen area. I saw that his fridge was covered in magnets so I went to inspect. They were all phallic in nature: the Empire State Building, a banana, the Washington Monument, a hot dog, a cactus. On the side were magnets of super hung, naked men. I didn't see this one coming.

"You all set? You want anything?" Matt asked upon joining me.

"What do you have?" My voice choked a little.

"I see you found my magnet collection. Funny, aren't they?"

"Hysterical," I said.

"Well," he said, opening his fridge. "I have lots of beer, there's Diet Coke, and I have wine."

"I'll have a beer." I don't know why I said that. I wanted wine. I didn't correct myself. What have I gotten myself into? I asked, looking around the apartment.

"Let's have a seat," he said. Directly in front of the television were two armchairs with a table in between them. It was an optimal viewing experience. I would expect no less from a Film Studies major. He took the large laser disc out of his sleeve and put it in the machine. He seemed so technologically advanced. I mean, I thought I was pretty cutting edge with my own VCR. He told me if I liked the film, he would make me a VHS copy. I might take him up on that, I thought.

Throughout the film, Matt continued to offer me another beer, which I took him up on. He always grabbed another for himself. I was mesmerized by the film. It left me uncomfortable and sad. And I was drunk. Muting the T.V., he came around to where I was sitting. On his knees, he started to rub my crotch. I leaned in and he kissed me. Within seconds, we were naked.

"Wait," he said, pausing mid-kiss. "Let me put something on." I thought he meant a condom. He took a disc from the stack on the desk and put it into the player. Two young, hairless guys were doing on screen, what I hoped be doing soon. I never understood putting on porn during sex. I mean, I'm not present to watch T.V. It's kind of an either/or scenario for me. But, he was into it, so I went with it.

As soon as we were done, he shut the T.V. off. I washed up and asked if I could spend the night, avoiding a drive home. He agreed and pulled out the futon. "I usually just sleep on it like a sofa."

"So do I!" I concurred.

Thanks to the alcohol, I fell asleep right away. I usually can't sleep in new environments. In the morning, Matt made us coffee and waffles. We sat at his little bistro table in his kitchen and quietly enjoyed our breakfast. "I have a gift for you," he said, handing me a VHS tape. "I made it while we slept." *Eraserhead* scribbled on the label with a Sharpie.

"Thank you! This is amazing." I was stoked to have my own copy. It was a film I definitely needed to see again. Sober.

We made plans to see each other the following weekend. I had work and he had school. We did email back and forth, however, throughout the week. Our third date played out exactly like the previous with the following updates: we ordered in and *Eraserhead* was replaced with *Blue Velvet*. When it came time to reenact our sex scene, Matt put the same porno DVD back in the player.

The next morning, I had to ask as I ate my waffles. "What's with the porn?"

"What do you mean?" he seemed startled by this question, despite the fact we were surrounded by pornography and pornographic images. He turned bright red.

"I, uh," he stuttered. "I can't...you know...without it." For someone so into nude imagery, he couldn't even say the word.

"You mean cum?" He nodded and stared at me, waiting for the judgment. Outwardly, I didn't. Internally, I was running as fast as I could from this guy.

"Is that a problem?" he asked, already knowing the answer. It was right there on my face. We finished our waffles and I went home with my new copy of *Blue Velvet*.

Kitty
(Memory #36)

Roads' End offered onsite classes taught by a UW-Platteville professor and if we received a B or better, the class was paid for by Roads' End and we received college credit. I was going to take full advantage of this knowing that I was going to design school. I settled on *Photography 101*. I had always loved photography and had taken a class in high school. I wasn't really any good at it but figured it was like a code that I just needed access to and I could crack it.

The classes met in Building 5, the corporate offices. I arrived early and took my seat at the front of the class. There was a strikingly beautiful woman with short salt and pepper hair standing next to the dry erase board. She had on dangly aquamarine earrings that I wondered if she made herself.

"How y'all doin'?" she asked as I entered.

"I'm well. And you?"

"I'm doin' just great, sugar." This made me smile. "What part a the company ya work for?"

"I'm in Corporate Sales. I work in the CAD department. But, that's not my life's work. I'm going to go to school in New York to be a designer."

"That's amazing," she said. Instantly, a connection was formed.

Her name was Kitty. She was a Texan transplant in Wisconsin. She got a job at the UW and moved there to be with her girlfriend, until said girlfriend cheated on her and left her. Kitty was unlike any lesbian I had ever encountered, what they called a lipstick lesbian. She was tall, trim, dressed to the nines and always had a full face of makeup on and smelled like a gardenia flower. She didn't even own a truck!

As it turned out, she lived in Mineral Point, on High Street a block down from my apartment. Her apartment was great. It was above the hardware store, in this old loft style space. I often thought how does such a space exist there? She had painted every surface glossy white, the trim, the doors, and the floors. Everything. She then added pops of color in her furniture, pillows and artwork.

Often, after work, I would head over to her place for beers and conversation. Some nights, we'd just watch *Seinfeld* and not talk. She definitely helped combat the loneliness I felt on a regular basis. She helped drag me out of my shell a bit, too. On one such occasion, we went to an estate sale. I would never go to one, but it was so much fun. I saw this amazing set of mid-century modern china in perfect condition. It had grey, black and brick red lines, triangles and circles in a border around the white coupe plates. She threw my hand in the air when it came time to bid on them. It all felt so dangerous. I ended up winning the set for five dollars. I still have and use them to this day.

I reprised my raspberry chicken recipe, serving it alongside a pile of couscous as a thank you dinner and to have our first of many meals on the china. Kitty brought the wine.

"Darlin' aren't you glad you got this china?" she said inspecting a cup and saucer.

"Yes, thank you."

"I love estate sales. I love to look at people's old stuff and imagine the stories connected to them." She made junk sound like heirlooms. I sat down beside her and we ate. After dinner, we walked down to the new ice cream shop that opened and she treated us to ice cream cones.

"Fall in love with light!" she would say at us in class, reviewing our photographs. "Fall in love with composition! Tell me a story! Make me ask questions!" She was so passionate about photography. Unfortunately for her, the class was largely comprised of middle-aged housewives looking for a craft project. This wasn't it.

"Thank God, you're in the class." Kitty said to me as we walked to our cars in the parking not. "Someone actually took photos of her Beanie Baby collection." I knew who the culprit was. "Can you believe that?"

"Look where you are!" I said, making a sweeping gesture with my hand.

"I know," she in a pouty voice. I never brought up the ex-girlfriend or why she stayed on. She always spoke about Austin, Texas as if it were the Promised Land. I wondered why she didn't return.

Kitty was incredibly supportive of my moving to New York for design school. At every chance she got, she would buy fashion related books for me. Thanks to her, I had assembled quite the canon of design and inspiration books. After I moved, I fell out of touch with her. I asked about her one time I was back there for a visit and was told she ended up moving back to Austin.

I got an A in photography.

Ahead of the Curve
(Memory #37)

I agreed to meet Steven at the Elvehjem Museum of Art on UW-Madison's campus. I wandered through the main space, drenched in light from the skylight above. I was so excited to meet him. He was a freshman, studying Biology. Younger than most of the guys I dated, I said why not. He was into me. That was pretty much the only prerequisite I had to dating.

I saw him but pretended not to. He was wearing a black leather jacket, black faded jeans, gold wireframe glasses and a mound of careless sandy blond hair. I could see him approaching me.

"Kyle?" he asked, leaning in a little.

"Steven?" I asked, knowing the answer. I could see a bouquet of white tulips in his hands. He hugged me and handed them to me. We nervously walked around the main floor gallery, stealing glances of each other when we pretended to look at the paintings.

"What do you want to do?" he whispered.

"Let's head outside so we can talk." He followed me out into the brisk Wisconsin air. My skin felt dry and itchy. "There," I said, now that we could talk above a whisper. "What do you want to do?"

"I know this is forward, but I'd really like to see where you're from. I'm always trapped here on campus. No car." I found this adorable and relatable.

"Are you sure? There's really not much to do there."

"I'd welcome that!"

"Ok! But, I warned you!" He laughed. I liked his laugh. We started walking towards the Rabbit. I was eager to get back inside someplace warm. I gave him control of the radio as I zipped down University Avenue. He chose the oldies station. I don't know why, but we both started singing along. I set the tulips in the cup holder between us. I never had any beverage in the car for fear of wearing it. That being said, I thought it was odd I could hear a soda bottle rolling back and forth behind my seat.

We were both singing along to *Paint It Black*. His hand found mine on top of the shifter and we locked pinkies. I smiled. His hand stayed with mine until almost to the city line. We didn't really say much for the car ride. He just looked out the window and smiled. I could tell he was happy to be out in the country. I was happy to have company. The Doors played on the radio.

Soon, we pulled off the highway, through town and into my driveway. I stopped the car just outside of my apartment. "This is it," I announced.

"I love it," he said. I wasn't sure if he did or was just being polite.

"Oh, shit." I realized I have no food in the house. "You mind if we stop at the grocery store?"

"Of course. And maybe we could rent a movie?"

"Sure," I said. I grabbed the soda bottle from behind my seat, opened my car door and set it next to the garage. "I'll throw that away later."

At the grocery store, we walked up and down each aisle, not being able to agree on any dinner options. Frozen pizza was the one thing we had in common. I grabbed a Tombstone pizza from the freezer case and we walked to the video rentals.

"Oh, man. Have you seen this film? It's one of my favorites." It was *All About Eve*.

"Sadly, I've missed that one. But it's on my list." They didn't have it at Dick's but did at the IGA? Weird.

Back at my apartment, I turned up the heat and put the pizza in the oven. There was no real insulation underneath my carpet. I think the carpet was actually applied directly to the cement floor. I offered Steven slippers, but he said he was fine. I wasn't so I put them on.

I cut the pizza into equal wedges and handed Steven his plate. I put the tape in the VCR and pressed play.

"Who's the Marilyn Monroe wannabe?" I asked, taking a bite of my pizza.

"That *is* Marilyn Monroe," he corrected me. I could feel my face flush. I paused the movie.

"Do you want anything to drink? I have wine, gin and I think vodka."

"Maybe a little wine." I went and poured us both giant glasses. "Whoa!" he said as I handed it to him.

After the movie (which I loved), he inched closer to me. And closer. He put his hand on my leg and started to rub it gently. I could make out a giant bulge under his jeans. He leaned in and our lips met. For 19, he was a great kisser. I gently fell backwards onto the futon, pulling him on top of me. I couldn't stop thinking about the bulge between us. I ran my hands up under his t-shirt and caressed his back. He moaned with pleasure.

I pulled his shirt up over his head and flung it on the floor. I kissed his neck as he wrestled my shirt loose from my chinos. He fell on me and we kissed some more. I held him like a delicate object next to me, not wanting to break it yet not wanting to let go of it. He sat up and unbuttoned my chinos and slid them and my boxers off in one motion. I was in heaven.

"Come here," I whispered, pulling him in so I could finally unbutton those jeans. He helped me by kicking them off. I then pulled down his navy boxer briefs to reveal what I had been waiting for. His penis, while beautiful, was completely curved to the right. Almost like a perfect U-turn sign. If that were straight, it would be massive! I said to myself. Then it dawned on me, where and how would that thing work? I awkwardly stroked him and I could feel a gob of pre-cum in my hand. He quivered and moaned and more oozed out onto my hand. I knew this was going to be easy. He flopped back down on me and dry humped me for a minute and then slumped down. I could feel his cum dripping down my arm. I pressed it to my side to avoid getting any on the futon.

After my turn, we got up and showered together. He didn't say a word. It was late and I was tired and didn't read too much into it. The next morning, he didn't say much either. We got in the car and I drove him back to campus. I asked if he wanted to stop someplace and get breakfast, my treat, but he declined. He kissed me quickly and jumped out of the car. I watched him disappear into a brown, drab, brick building.

Pulling back into my driveway, I noticed the soda bottle, frozen next to the garage. I picked it up and put it in the bin under the sink. I logged into my email to see if Steven had written. He did! I clicked the message open.

> *Kyle,*
>
> *Thank you for last night. However, I cannot see you again. I cannot be with someone who doesn't respect Mother Earth.*
>
> *Steven*

I looked at the cabinet under the sink and shook my head. "Yeah, well, I can't date anyone with a deformed dick," I wrote and immediately deleted it. "Kids," I said out loud and shook my head again.

Take That

It had been forever since I had both seen Anka and been to downtown Madison. She was now living with her boyfriend and I wanted to meet him as well. Thanksgiving was the following day and I had already seen everyone in my family that I needed to.

"Sparky!" I said as she came into view on State Street.

"Evol!" she returned and I hugged her. "This is Derek."

"Pleased to meet you," I said, shaking his hand. They had been dating for four years. "So, where do you want to go?"

"Let's go to The Great Dane," Derek suggested. We started trekking towards the Capital.

Along the way, Derek told me about his work that he was doing at a medical research firm. Both of them were wildly passionate about music. Knowing this, I asked about the various concerts they had been to. Most of the bands I hadn't heard of. I felt out of touch.

"What do you do?" asked Derek. My heart sank. I should have been prepared for this question, but it blindsided me.

"Well, I'm currently not employed."

"Oh, man. Sorry." I could see the embarrassment on his face.

"No sweat. I'll figure it out," I said, trying to reassure us both.

We found three open stools at the bar and got settled. Anka looked radiant. She always did, but there was a new glow about her. I was happy that she had Derek. I always felt protective of her.

Our beer order placed, Derek announced that he was paying for the tab and that we were going to eat as well. I was ok with this. We each ordered a different burger and ate without speaking, focused on the delicious food in front of us.

"Evol, I have something to tell you," Anka said, breaking the silence.

"Ok," I said, braced for the news.

"Derek and I are getting married." I have never seen her look so happy.

"Oh, my God! Congratulations!" I hugged them both. "When is the date? You know I'm coming back to Wisconsin for the wedding!"

"Next June," Derek said. I put the date in my iPhone.

"You're the first person I've told," Anka said.

"And, we were wondering if you would be in the wedding party," said Derek.

"Of course I will! You guys! This is such great news!" We had another round of beers and Anka laid out the wedding plans. Normally, weddings and babies do nothing for me and I avoid the subjects at all costs. But, this was Anka we were talking about.

Outside, I hugged them both goodbye and wished them a Happy Thanksgiving. They headed off towards East Wilson Street and I walked back towards the Capital.

Wow, I thought. I tucked my hands into my peacoat to warm them. My Anka is getting married. I was both happy for her and jealous of her at the same time. I sighed and rounded the corner by the Inn On The Park. A familiar face came into view.

"Kyle?" said the familiar face. My heart dropped into my stomach. This was exactly the type of chance encounter I wanted to avoid on this trip.

"Evan! Wow! What a surprise." We awkwardly hugged.

"What has it been? Eight? Nine years?"

"Something like that," I said, putting my hands back into my peacoat. "What are you up to now?"

"I'm the chef here," he said pointing at the Inn On The Park. "What about you?"

"I'm just here, visiting the family for Thanksgiving."

"I have to run, need prep for dinner service."

"No, I understand." He looked the same, I thought. I was suddenly aware of how I've aged.

"Say, would you want to get together tonight after my shift? Would be great to reconnect." He said 'reconnect' in such a way that it was dirty and sexual.

"I'd love that," I said. "Where and when?"

"We can meet here. There's a new restaurant near the lake that's open all night. I'll get us a reservation."

"Perfect," I said, hugging him goodbye. I watched him turn back and wave at me before he entered the hotel. He seemed so genuinely happy to see me. The memories of that summer with him flooded over me. The first kiss, the plans for the future, the nights above the restaurant and of course, the trip.

I got in the Rabbit and went back to Grandma's house. I didn't meet Evan at our scheduled time. Take that, I thought.

It's a Small, Small World
(Memory #38)

"I'm Kyle," I said, extending my hand to this tall, strikingly beautiful Middle Eastern woman.

"I'm Leda," she said. "Please, sit."

"Thank you," I said, taking a seat at the design worktable at Roads' End. I had decided to put together a portfolio of my work and apply to design school in New York. I discovered Leda on the company's Intranet, as she was the lead designer for women's tailored clothing and studied at F.I.T., where I was applying.

"How can I help you?" she asked, taking a sip from her Starbucks cup.

"I'd like to show you my portfolio and get your feedback. And, if it's not asking too much, I'd love a letter of recommendation."

"No problem! Let's take a look at what you've got." I opened the large black fake leather case for her and started to explain why I had drawn or sewn each piece. She pointed to a bright orange and fuchsia paisley dress I designed. "That reminds me of a time at Ralph Lauren when I wore a similar print pajama type pant to work and Ralph loved them and had to do a version." I smiled at her story. Maybe I would have such stories one day.

Leda and I worked on and off for a good two weeks to

refine and edit my portfolio. I would sneak away to Building 5 on my lunch hours to meet with her. I was really pleased the with end result and owed so much of it to her keen, refined eye. She wrote a glowing letter of recommendation, saying that I was an old soul, brimming with ideas. That made my day. I neatly packaged everything and FedEx'd it to F.I.T.

Three weeks later, I saw the envelope in my mailbox. It contained more than one piece of paper. This was a great sign. They wouldn't send a multiple page rejection letter. I opened it. I was in. I sat down on the edge of the futon and cried. The sinking ship that was my life could be saved. Turned around and avoid hitting that iceberg.

I called Leda first to tell her of the news. She wanted to take me out to dinner and drinks to celebrate. I then went to the library and told the librarian of my news. She had special ordered patternmaking books from another library for me. I had to tell her.

That night I walked down High Street to the bottom of the hill to The Chesterfield Inn. It was this quaint, tiny little restaurant set in a beautiful limestone building. It was owned by a restaurant group in Madison and was deemed by the locals as the "fancy" restaurant in town. It was the site of many anniversary and birthday dinners. They had a beautiful terrace between the stony hill and the building.

"Hi, I'm meeting someone here," I said to the girl standing at the podium outside of the terrace.

"Are you meeting inside or on the terrace?" she asked.

"Terrace." She led me around the back and I could see Leda sitting at the table with man, his hair slicked back. Must be her husband, I thought. "Hi, Leda," I said approaching them.

"Kyle! Congratulations!" she said and hugged me. "I'd like you to meet my husband." He turned and stood up. It was Rob, married and lonely Rob. We had slept together two days earlier. My face went white.

"Pleased to meet you," I said.

"Pleased to meet you," he said, shaking my hand. I took my seat opposite them both. I couldn't believe that I was having an affair with my mentor's husband. I could only imagine what karmic repercussions were in store for me. Did she not mention me to him? How did she explain why I was at dinner? Did she not use my name?

I made it through dinner without issue. Wine helped. Immensely. I thanked them both for dinner and thanked Leda again for all her help and support. Walking back up High Street, I felt ashamed. I thought of Leda, trusting, helpful, kind Leda. I never saw Rob again after that dinner. Neither of us contacted the other. We knew it was over.

Thanksgiving Day

"Will you go up to Walmart and get some more chicken stock?" Mom asked from the kitchen. I was in the living room, sitting next to the fireplace, warming up.

"Sure," I said. I put on my peacoat and grabbed my car keys from the table by the door. There was a layer of mist across the windshield of the Rabbit. I longed to be back by the fire. The chill in the air was the kind that sunk deep within, to the bone. Maybe I was just getting old, I thought. My grandma could pretty much predict any weather phenomenon by her joints. Maybe I had inherited that gift.

Walmart was only a few minutes away and was sure to be open. I had a love/hate relationship with Walmart. When I was living alone in Mineral Point, I would drive there after work and look through the fabric department. They always had dollar-a-yard fabric. I would buy enough to complete whatever sewing project was interesting me at the moment. There was always this little bitty thing named Eunice who worked in the department, cutting and folding bolts of fabric. She would always ask what I was making this time. When I got accepted into F.I.T., I made a special trip to Walmart to tell her.

I parked the car as close as I could. Looked like half the town was there as well. I thought of my apartment back in New York. I wondered what my friend Jack was up to, hoping he was watering my plants like he said he would.

There it is, I said to myself, that 'Walmart' smell. They

all smelled the same. I couldn't really describe it, but I knew it instantly. I hoped that no one would recognize me and ask me how things were. I didn't feel like filling anyone in. I loathed small talk more than anything. And I was horrible at it.

I headed for the grocery section and found an endcap of nothing but chicken stock. I grabbed a couple cans and turned to leave when I decided to drop in on Eunice. She was probably at home preparing Thanksgiving dinner for her family, but maybe she decided to pick up an extra shift. I found the fabric section completely empty. "Eunice?" I called out. No answer. I turned to leave when I noticed her picture taped to the column beside the cutting table. "In loving memory," it said. My lip trembled.

"Kyle?" a familiar voice said.

"Oh, my God! Hi!" I said to Susan. Her son, Marc, was a year younger than me and also gay. We had fooled around all throughout high school. We never kissed. He wouldn't. And we never did anal. I wouldn't. It was pretty much two awkward teens getting off together.

"I am so glad to see you! Your mother said you'd be in town." Of course she did.

"How are you? Working here now?" There had been a round of layoffs at Road's End where she had worked for ten years.

"Yup," she said, tugging at her royal blue smock.

"How's Marc?" Why did I ask? I didn't want to know

the answer to that question. I knew the answer to that question. He was great, successful law career, perfectly partnered, still maintaining his trim body. I was suddenly self-conscious of my stomach.

"He's great. Working on some case in Abu Dhabi."

"Wow, that's great!"

"What about you?" I had just lost my job. I didn't want to talk about it. So, I lied. I said everything was fine. I didn't want word getting back to Marc that I was unhappy, single and jobless. I made my departure as quickly as I could and paid for the chicken stock.

"Why did you not tell me Eunice died?" I said as I entered mom's house, not yet taking off my jacket.

"I don't know, I guess it slipped my mind." Seriously? She was constantly calling me to tell me of someone's passing, almost always someone that I did not know. Here was a death I cared about. I felt suddenly empty. "Say, can you go back and get cranberry sauce?"

"Seriously? Why didn't you call my cell?"

"I didn't think of it until now."

"Did you buy a turkey?"

"Go on," she said, throwing a twenty-dollar bill at me.

Back at Walmart, I found a display of canned cranberry sauce. I preferred fresh sauce, but my family liked the jellied, canned kind. I grabbed two cans and headed back to the checkout. The clerk was this squat, balding guy who looked like he had a major case of pink eye. I threw a bottle of hand sanitizer on the conveyor belt. Outside, I coated my hands with it.

"Kyle?!" a voice made its way to me.

"Hi," I said. It was Mary, a family friend. She wrapped her arms around me.

"So good to see you! Back in town I see."

"Yup."

"Where are you working these days?" she asked with a smile. Ugh. I pulled out my usual lie and she bought it. Luckily, the mist had turned into rain and she said goodbye quickly and ran into Walmart. Inside my car, I put my head on the steering wheel and cried.

You Can't Go Back Again

The day after Thanksgiving, I called up Adam to see if he wanted to go drinking. He, of course, did. By this point, I had enough of my family and needed to escape to Madison to see a friend and consume alcohol without judgment.

I hopped in the Rabbit and headed off, as I had done so many times before. On the highway, I passed car after car, headed in the opposite direction, full of their various Black Friday deals. I pushed a cassette I had made for car rides into the player. The speakers crackled as the music started. I opened the moonroof and cranked the heat.

It had been a good two years since I had seen Adam. When I first moved to New York, and came home for Christmas, all of my Roads' End friends would meet at a bar and have a welcome back party for me. Each semester and year that passed became less of a production. Now, it had been distilled to the occasional drink or coffee to catch up.

I thought back to all the nights we'd go out drinking together after work. Middle aged soccer moms, Adam and myself. It was such an odd mix of personalities and I liked to think that I was the thread that bound them together. When my digitizing class graduated and started work, we were on the night shift. The day shift blamed all problems on the night shift and vice versa. When we moved up to the day shift, I was the first to break bread and join the regulars. Soon, I had repaired those bridges. And what better unifier is there than drinking and complaining about work?

We had our rotation of the four bars in Dodgeville that we'd frequent, each serving local beer and deep-fried cheese curds. I was always "fancy" because I ordered a martini. Stoli vodka, straight up with a lemon twist. Most times, I would have to walk the bartender through the making of the cocktail. They were used to pouring beers and mixing screwdrivers. My order always threw a curveball at them.

Laughter, smoke and stories would fill the air. People would break off into groups and share gripes and complaints about some injustice the management team was inflicting on us worker bees. I tried to avoid getting pulled into those conversations, but sometimes it was the only thing that helped one feel better. Adam and I were usually the last two to leave. Each convincing the other we were ok to drive. Not a good mixture.

Adam and I agreed to meet at Café Montmartre. I pulled the car into the parking garage and thought that Buon Gusto was just like Café Montmartre, except the martinis were better at Montmartre by far. Then I remembered that I only drank Campari and sodas at Buon Gusto and martinis at Café Montmartre. Glad I cleared that up, I thought with a chuckle.

Buttoning up my peacoat, I stepped out from the garage and crossed the street. My heart sank, as I looked the door. I could see Adam walking from the direction of State Street. I pointed at the door and shook my head.

"What? What's wrong?" he said hurrying up to see what I was pointing at, which was a sign on the door saying: "BUSINESS CLOSED." Our beloved Café

Montmartre looked so sad. We peered in through the windows to see that all of the dark wooden chairs and tables were removed. "Well, that fucking sucks," he said.

We turned and started walking towards State Street. We stopped at the first college dive bar we found. I thought back to all the memories I had back at Café Montmartre. I remembered the time that Harry and Tim set me up with someone they knew. They swore that David and I would be life partners. We met at the bar and I ordered a martini, he ordered a whiskey neat. I don't really remember much of that meeting, just a feeling I had that I was more into him than he was me. I was right.

I thought of the time that Jan and I spent the millennium there. They threw a black tie event. We bought tickets and I pulled out my tux. I made her this beautiful white satin button front shirt and long skirt to wear. We had the best time. Everyone looked great, was happy, drinking and eating and I was with my dear friend. It was exactly how I wanted to welcome in 2000.

"That place was so cool," said Adam, taking a sip of his Jameson.

"I know. I wonder why it closed." I thought of pulling out my iPhone and googling it, but decided against it. She was gone. I had to accept it. "What's new?" I asked him.

"I'm getting married." I choked on my martini at hearing this.

"What?"

"Yup. You're invited to the wedding."

"Which is when?" I was still in shock. Two bombshells dropped on me in a matter of fifteen minutes.

"Next summer."

"Wow."

"I know," he said, making eye contact with the bartender and pointing at his empty glass.

Madison always left me feeling sad. I could never exactly explain why. It was always an oasis from the confines of my hometown. It was the place where I went on dates, got laid and rejected. I never did have any success dating in Madison. It was the home of all of my friends whom I considered family, yet I never had the chance to live there. And it was always the point of entry and departure for whenever I visited from New York.

I ran my finger around the rim of my martini glass. Looking up, I saw the bartender standing there. "Yeah, I'll have another."

Reset Button
(Memory #39)

I completely forgot I had a personal ad out there. I had
been so focused on my upcoming move to New York
that I spent very little time online. I had arranged with
Grandma that I would store the Rabbit in her garage
and the bulk of my possessions in her attic.

I logged on and checked my email. There was an email
from someone I didn't recognize:

> *Dear Kyle,*
>
> *My name is Jesse. I recently moved back to
> Madison from New York. I was working as
> an attorney there. I really liked your profile
> and your picture. Let me know if you would
> like to get coffee sometime and connect.*
>
> *Best,*
> *Jesse*
>
> *P.S. Attached is my photo.*

And it was. And it was beautiful. I wrote him back and
explained that I would love to meet him, but in a few
weeks, I would no longer be living in the state. And
then I deleted the ad. Of course, no one would answer
my personal ad until I wasn't available. An hour later,
he wrote back and said he didn't care, that he still
wanted to meet me. He even offered to make the trek
to Mineral Point. I took him up on that.

The next day, at the appointed time, there was a knock on my front door. I opened to find Jesse standing there, framed in sunlight, holding a bunch of lilies that looked like they'd been picked from the bushes growing outside. Upon inspection, I realized that's exactly where they were from.

"I'm sorry! I totally forgot to get you flowers," he said, handing them to me.

"Thank you," I said, laughing. "And you don't have to get me flowers!" I welcomed him in and put the flowers in water. "Sorry about the mess. I'm packing up the place."

"So, I see," he said sitting down next to a box on the futon. I offered him a Diet Coke or something stronger. He took the soda. I opened one for me, too.

"Strange isn't it? You're back from New York and I'm moving there."

"Timing is everything isn't it?"

I laughed. "Yes, yes it is." An awkward silence fell between us. "So, tell me about your time in New York."

"Well, not much to tell really. After graduation, I took a position with a law firm there. It was never really my plan to live there. I did it more for the experience than anything. And then the firm went bust. I was thinking about what was next for me, you know? I could stay on the same path of criminal law or I could hit the reset button and do something different." I liked the sound of that. I could definitely relate. "So, I decided to work in environmental law and got a job at the UW and moved back."

"What was dating like in New York?" Probably not the best question to ask your date.

He laughed. "I'll let you form your own opinion." I liked him. He was so different than most of the guys that I met. He was without pretense and I found that so genuine and tender. He wasn't attractive in a way that would stop heads on the street, but the more we chatted, the sexier he became. I really liked that.

"Let me buy you dinner," he said. I wasn't going to argue with him. I suggested we go to a new café over in Dodgeville that had opened on Main Street. I had become a local again in Mineral Point and didn't want to run into people who knew me and would gossip about me being with a handsome stranger.

"Excellent choice," he said as we sat down at our table. The smell of fresh brewed coffee filled every corner of the place. The walls were lined with photographs from local artists. The menu was inspired as well. I went for the roasted lemon and garlic chicken; Jesse had the wild mushroom lasagna. I would have had that, but I had an irrational fear of mushrooms. I guess it was a texture thing.

"So, where in Madison are you living?" I asked, pushing the lemon down into my glass and poured Diet Coke over it.

"Well, I'm staying with my parents until I get my own place. They live in Sun Prairie. Where in New York will you be living?"

"On campus at F.I.T."

"That's a great area. It's gotten so much better the last couple of years." He was right. And in the time I lived there, it got even better. When Whole Foods moved in, I knew it was going to be great.

"When you moved to New York, did you know anyone? Have any family there?" I asked.

"No, not a soul."

"Same here."

"You'll do fine. If I can do it, anyone can." I smiled. He was so gentle and supportive. I couldn't fathom him working in criminal law. Back at my place, having put Duke Ellington in the CD player, I sat next to Jesse and asked him if he wanted a drink. He said yes, but I didn't get up. I fell into his arms and he planted one, tender kiss on my lips. "Thank you for tonight," he said, looking at me like he had seen the face of God.

"Thank you," I offered back. I moved in and kissed him. I could have sat there forever and kissed him.

"You want a massage?" he offered. I was used to just getting down to it. He was the real deal. I told him there was some body lotion in the cabinet in the bathroom. He returned with the Bath and Body Works bottle. "Take your shirt of and lie on your stomach," he said, almost in a whisper. He ran his hands across my chest hair and smiled. I did as he said.

The massage was so soothing and relaxing. When he was finished, I rolled over, exposing my hard-on. He ran his hand across it and came in for another kiss. I unbuttoned my chinos for him to go in and explore. Next, his clothes came off and our bodies intertwined.

"Now, I really should thank you," I said as he rolled off me. He laughed.

"I know it's not my place, but I really wish you weren't leaving," he said, again almost as a whisper.

"Or you would have stayed in New York."

"We probably wouldn't have met then." It was true. For whatever reason, we were brought together now. That's what was important.

After Jesse left, I continued boxing up memories, Duke Ellington still on the stereo. I packed up my sewing machine and serger. My two best friends. I neatly folded all the dresses, suit jackets, shirts and skirts I had made, each one telling a story and reminding me of where I was in my life and at as a designer.

The next day, I came home from work and saw there was something in my doorframe. I got out of the Rabbit and saw that it was a giant bouquet of the most beautiful flowers. I picked up the card. It was from Jesse.

Here's to hitting the reset button.

Hoarkin' Morton
(Memory #40)

"We wish you the best of luck in New York," said my boss, Cheryl, at Roads' End. "Know that you always have a home here," she said with a smile. And with that, my exit interview was done. As I left the conference room, several of my coworkers were there and hugged me goodbye. I set my final time sheet on the front desk and grabbed my bag. Moving in two days seemed a million light years away.

"See you tonight!" I said as I walked down the stairs to the front door one last time. My entire department was throwing me a goodbye party at Sunshine's house. Sunshine wasn't her real name. It's the name we gave Margie since she almost never smiled. I could get her to crack a smile or even a laugh on occasion. She said she'd host the party and make her famous Sloppy Joes. The only rule was that aside from the kitchen and bathroom, we'd stay in the backyard.

I drove down to Dick's and returned the last of my video rentals. I stopped in the liquor department and picked up two bottles of Stoli vodka, a bottle of vermouth and lemons. I would miss this place, I thought.

Around 7 P.M., I parked the Rabbit outside Sunshine's house. It was the typical midwestern ranch house. I could hear everyone out back. Rounding the corner, I saw a big bonfire and all my friends sitting around it on folding chairs. Jan, Adam, Sunshine, Layla, Tina, they were all there, drinks in hand. Paula Morton, another coworker of mine, arrived right behind me. I set my martini kit in the kitchen and grabbed a Sloppy Joe and joined my friends by the fire. Frank Sinatra's *New York, New York* played on a boom box.

"I can't believe you're leaving," said Adam.

"Well, I opened the door. The rest of you could just walk through it!" I was referring to work and the gripes we had. The group laughed.

"I'm going to miss seeing you all every day. The reality hasn't set in. I don't think it will until I'm off the plane."

After finishing my sandwich, I offered to make martinis. Jan accepted. She followed me into the kitchen. "I have something for you," she said extending her hand, her blue eyes twinkling with glee.

"I said no presents!" I said taking the little box from her hand. "Unless it's cash." She laughed. I opened the box to find a little silver compass.

"So you don't lose your way," she said, fighting back tears. I hugged her and handed her a martini.

"Thank you." Rejoining the group, we teased Greg for bringing the Mormon intern to a cocktail party. She blushed and sipped her bottled water. We went around the circle and told our favorite moments together. This type of gathering should happen more often, I thought. I got choked up a few times, but kept the tears at bay.

After everyone had food and a few drinks, people

dispersed into smaller groups. I would float from island to island of mini conversations. Soon, I went from tipsy to drunk. Everyone was wasted. I sat and warmed my hands by the roaring fire. I wondered what life would be like in New York City. Talk about the polar opposite of this existence.

I decided to wash away those thoughts with another martini. I stood up, stretched and picked up my empty glass. I saw Sunshine storming out of her house. Her husband, Adam and Tina went running behind her. I tried to make sense of the situation. Before I could, the image of Paula appeared in the door. Her white t-shirt, chin and neck were covered with bright orange Sloppy Joe vomit. She looked like she was about to pass out.

I didn't see it with my own eyes, but was told that Paula barfed all over Sunshine's brand new cream-colored sofa, which she bought two days earlier. Someone called Paula's brother who came and cleaned her up and took her over to his place to sleep it off.

"Of all the surfaces she could fucking vomit on!" I could hear Sunshine screaming.

Sunshine had two different companies come clean the sofa with no success. She ended up burning it at the next bonfire and bought a new one. She also stopped throwing parties. I haven't had a Sloppy Joe since that party. Paula, from that moment on, was forever known as *Hoarkin' Morton*.

Father Figure

"You should go say goodbye to your father," Grandma said as we sat around her kitchen table, watching an old episode of *Bonanza*.

"I know," I said, not taking my eyes from the set. It's not that I was riveted to the show. I was hoping the conversation wouldn't continue.

"You two need to make an effort," she pressed.

"I know," I repeated. She lit a cigarette and unwrapped a piece of sugar-free candy. I finished the last of my Diet Coke.

"Hey there," she said into her cellphone. "Just checking to see if you're home…Ok…We'll be up in a bit." My dad lived up the road from Grandma's farm. "Your dad's home. We'll head up there in a few minutes."

I put on my peacoat and slipped into my loafers. Grandma put on her coat and grabbed the keys to the truck. The Rabbit had been packed away again, in her garage, until the next visit. That is, if she lasted that long. Rust had taken over her exterior like a cancer.

Dad and his wife lived in the standard ranch house, the kind that you knew the floor plan just by looking at it. They built it on a small piece of land that used to be part of Grandma's cornfield. She sold the parcel to them and then rented out the rest to the farmer further up the road. I could hear the gravel crunch under the truck tires as she pulled into his driveway.

She parked behind the house and we walked up the wooden stairs to the deck and into the kitchen through the sliding doors. Dad and Bonnie were sitting in matching reclining chairs, watching *Wheel of Fortune*.

"What's the good word?" Grandma said as she sat down on their powder blue sofa.

"Mmmm. Not much," Dad said, not taking his eyes off the T.V. We all sat there in silence, watching Vanna touch the rectangles as they lit up. "So, you heading back tomorrow?" He turned to me.

"Yup. Time to head back," I said.

"You have a nice trip?" asked Bonnie, lighting a cigarette. Dad already had one lit, as did Grandma. I was the lone non-smoker in the room. My eyes were burning and I found it hard to breathe.

"Yeah, it was nice to be back."

"Jumping Rope!" Grandma blurted out at the T.V. with pride. She was right. She could have won a new Hyundai. I pictured her in it and laughed. "What? I got it right!"

"I know," I said.

"What time's your flight?" Bonnie asked while changing the channel to *CSI*.

"Tomorrow afternoon at 4."

"Oh, that's not so bad," she said. They had seen the episode before. She outlined the plot for me. I nodded. No one spoke as we all watched the show. I was on my iPhone, texting Sydney back in New York. She was having boyfriend trouble. To me, that was way more interesting.

"Where are the boys?" Grandma asked. She was referring to Bonnie's kids from her first marriage. They were much younger than my brother and I.

"Oh, they are with their father," she said, lighting another cigarette. I am going to have to dry clean my coat, I thought. "You guys want a pop?" she offered us. Grandma took a Diet Pepsi. I declined. "You sure?" Finally, I agreed to one as well. We watched another episode or some variant of *CSI* while they continued to smoke.

"Well, we should probably head back down the road," Grandma said, I stood immediately and grabbed my coat.

"It was so nice seeing you," said Bonnie.

"You too," I said as I hugged her. I then hugged my dad. "Good seeing you, Dad."

"You too," he said. Grandma was crying. She always got emotional at goodbyes.

As we climbed back in the truck, I could see Dad and Bonnie waving at us from the sliding glass doors. I waved back.

"Sure good seeing you two together," Grandma said,

still wiping away tears. She desperately wanted us to be close. We weren't going to be and I was ok with that. I made peace with that fact years ago. That ship with my brother and I had long sailed away. He was actually a very attentive father to Bonnie's two boys. At first I was jealous and then I realized, for him, late was better than never.

Power Up
(Memory #41)

In preparation for design school, I needed a new computer. The old Apple Performa I had was fine, but was five years old and starting to show her age. I wanted a computer that I could take to class or with me when I returned home on breaks. I decided to buy a PowerBook. I saved up money (which for me is no easy feat) and bought it. I stood beneath posters of Gandhi, Madame Curie, and Pablo Picasso, each urging me to Think Different, as I waited for the sales associate to bring me my shiny new laptop.

I couldn't wait to drive home and unbox the computer and get designing. Adam had recently upgraded his computer to a Power Mac. Ever since that time, we've pretty much upgraded Apple computers at the same time. He always opts for the desktop, and I a laptop.

I transferred my files over and shut down the Performa one last time. I found someone online who would buy it from me for $250. Not bad, I thought.

I began making the rounds to all my friends and family to say goodbye. Teary eyed, they all wished me well. They knew that there wasn't much for me in Wisconsin and that my dreams and goals were different than would be found there. We all secretly knew that I wasn't moving back after college. My mom held out hope that I would return to work at Roads' End. That never happened.

"I can't believe you're leaving," said Adam at a bar on Main Street in Darlington, where he lived. I had a 9:30

A.M. flight to La Guardia the following morning.

"I can't either. There's been so much planning and talk of it, now that it's here, I can't believe it." Adam ordered a Jameson for himself and a martini for me. I had to explain to the bartender how to make it. He didn't have a proper martini glass, so it got served to me in a plastic margarita glass.

"What are you going to do?" I asked him as we sipped our drinks.

"I'm thinking about moving to Madison and getting a job in graphic design. Maybe take some classes." There was a rumor circulating that the CAD department at Roads' End was going to shrink, with most of the work being farmed out to India. Only a handful of staff would be kept on to make corrections and repairs. This eventually did come true.

"Cool," I said. Hank Williams played on the stereo.

"So, let's see it," he said, referring to my new PowerBook. I took it out of the carrying case and handed it to him. He played around on it, opening various programs, while I drank my martini. Was I going to make the kind of friends in New York that I had in Wisconsin? Would we stay in touch? Would they all forget about me? Replace me? What if a new, even more fabulous gay guy moves into southwest Wisconsin, filling the void I left?

"You going to get a mouse?" Adam asked, not taking his eyes off the screen, as he dragged his finger across the trackpad.

"Yeah, I think so. I like the idea of not having one, but I'm just so used to it." I ordered us another round of drinks. I was going to miss him, I thought. After twenty minutes, Adam closed the lid and slid the computer back to me. He then took a card out of his jacket and slid it in my direction.

"Don't open it here," he said, not looking at me. I wondered what was in the card, if he was tearing up.

I settled the tab and Adam walked me to my car and hugged me goodbye. I watched him in the rear view mirror as he walked to his car. When he was out of sight, I opened the card. It read:

> *Kyle,*
> *I will miss you. A lot.*
> *Adam*

A prepaid calling card fell out and landed in my lap. I started crying. I sat in the Rabbit a good fifteen minutes and cried. When it was out of my system, I started the car and drove home.

The following morning, I zipped shut my suitcases and put my PowerBook in my messenger bag. My aunt picked me up from my grandma's to take me to the airport. My grandma and Mom lined up and hugged me goodbye, both of them crying. Mom told me to have a nice life as she had done once before. The comment was just as bizarre as the first time hearing it.

Aunt Pam and I met Phaedra at the Sunprint Café on Midvale. She already had plans to visit me in New York the following month. That made leaving somehow easier, knowing there would be a familiar face there soon enough.

Pam pulled the car over at the airport and helped me unload my two suitcases. I kissed her cheek and thanked her for taking me to the airport. It was much less emotional or drama-filled than if my mom took me. I grabbed my bags and headed into the airport, setting in motion the next chapter of my life.

Until Next Time

Mom honked as she pulled in the driveway at my grandmother's house. Grandma's eyes filled up with tears. Mine did too. I hugged her and grabbed my suitcase. From the car, I waved back at her, she was crying. It broke my heart that she was so lonely. I know that feeling all too well.

"I can't believe your trip is over already. I barely got to see you," Mom said as I buckled my seatbelt.

"I know. It went by so fast."

"Did you have a nice time?"

"Yeah, it was good to see everyone." I wasn't ready to return to New York. Not that there were any great opportunities for me in Wisconsin, but being around my family, for all their issues, was comforting. I turned on the heated seat function and rubbed my hands together.

"Where do you want to have lunch?"

"You can pick," I said, looking at the frosted, rolling hills and the cows wandering on them.

"Let's go to The Olive Garden. I just love that place." Suddenly, I was ready to return to New York, if for the pizza alone. I smiled at Mom and returned my focus to the countryside. Those cows must be freezing, I thought. And yet there they were, wandering around with their tails flopping back and forth.

When we arrived at The Olive Garden at West Towne

Mall, my mom announced she had a surprise for me. It was four blocks of aged sharp cheddar cheese, my favorite. I laughed at her present and neatly arranged them in my suitcase. It was cold enough out that I didn't have to worry about damaging my dairy gifts. I hugged her and thanked her for being a stereotype. She laughed at me.

"What are you going to have?" she asked, not looking up from her laminated menu.

"Just the salad and breadsticks."

"That's it? Go on. Get something, whatever you like." The server came and my mom ordered fettuccine alfredo with grilled chicken. I stuck to my original order. "So, what is your plan?" she asked, taking a sip from her Diet Coke. Again, the dreaded question.

"I don't know. Get a job, I guess."

"That's it? Get a job?"

"Mom, please. You can't begin to know the toll this has taken on my self-esteem." I felt completely broken down and gun shy. The server set down the big acrylic bowl of salad and fake wood breadbasket. I helped myself to a breadstick.

"Here," she said as she slid two one hundred-dollar bills across the table.

"What's this for?"

"To help you out. I know how expensive it is out there." I put the money in my pocket and remembered that was the exact amount of money that I moved to New York with. Funny that that was the amount I was returning with.

"Thank you," I said, not looking at her. We enjoyed the rest of our lunch without mention of my employment troubles. Just talk of who was dating who, who died, who was sleeping with who. Small town gossip never really did it for me. I didn't care though; at least the conversation wasn't directed at me.

After lunch, she bought me a new pair of shoes at Banana Republic. Then, we got on the Beltline and headed to the east side to the airport. Mom pulled the car over and we both hopped out. I took my suitcase from the backseat. She hugged me and started crying.

"Have a safe flight," she said as I started wheeling my bag inside the airport. "I love you."

"Love you, too, Mom." I checked in at the computerized terminal, put my bag on the conveyor belt and went upstairs to security. On the other side, I sat on the faux brown leather bench and watched a plane slowly taxi towards the gate. I didn't really feel like reading or listening to music as I usually did to kill time. There were too many thoughts swirling around in my head. The question I kept coming back to was what's next?

"Attention passengers, we are now boarding all zones for United flight UA1554 with nonstop service to Newark Liberty International Airport," boomed from the loudspeaker and I grabbed my bag. The line moved quickly and I soon found myself at the entrance. I put my hand on the side of the plane and thought, until next time.

The End

About the Author

Jamie Godfrey is author and entrepreneur. When he is not jotting down his quirky musings, he is the owner/designer of Jamie Godfrey Home Collection. There he sells a range of handmade home goods. Dairyland is Jamie's second novel. He currently lives in Jersey City, NJ.

www.ingramcontent.com/pod-product-compliance
Lightning Source LLC
Chambersburg PA
CBHW031511040426
42445CB00009B/171